Eva Jiricna

Design in Exile

WITH MANY
THANKS
SINCERELY

Eva

A Blueprint Monograph
Published by Fourth Estate
and Wordsearch

Eva Jiricna

Design in Exile

Martin Pawley

Blueprint Monographs
Ron Arad Restless Furniture
Deyan Sudjic
Nigel Coates The City in Motion
Rick Poynor
Rei Kawakubo and Comme des Garçons
Deyan Sudjic

First published in Great Britain in 1990 by Fourth Estate Ltd, 289 Westbourne Grove, London W11 2QA in conjunction with Blueprint magazine, 26 Cramer Street, London W1M 3HE

Copyright © 1990 Martin Pawley, Fourth Estate and Wordsearch Publishing

British Library Cataloguing in Publication Data
Pawley, Martin
Eva Jiricna. - (Blueprint monographs)
1. Architectural design.
Jiricna, Eva
I. Title II. Series
720.92

ISBN 1-872180-16-7

Design: Esterson Lackersteen
Series editor: Vicky Wilson
Cover and chapter divider photographs: Phil Sayer
Colour reproduction: Precise Litho Ltd
Printed in Great Britain by E. G. Bond Ltd

Acknowledgments
This book is based on a number of conversations with Eva Jiricna held in the spring and summer of 1990. Occasional participants included Jon Tollit, Gillian Gould and other members of the staff of EJA. I am particularly indebted to Gillian Gould for helping with research and documentation.
Martin Pawley

Photographic credits
Alan and Sylvia Blanc 12, 35. Richard Bryant/Arcaid 38, 39, 40, 41, 42, 43, 64, 66, 67, 70, 74, 82/3, 87, 91, 94/5, 98, 99. Martin Charles 44, 45. Jeremy Cockayne 71. Peter Cook 54, 55, 56, 57, 58/9, 64, 65, 67, 68, 69. Prudence Cuming Associates 19. Richard Davies 100. John Harland 20. Eddie Ryle-Hodges 21. Alistair Hunter 46, 47, 48, 49, 50, 51, 79. Ivan Nemec 52. Sharon Risedorph 53, 54. Phil Sayer 2, 8, 24, 36, 72, 96,108. The images on pages 10, 11, 26, 27, 28, 30, 31, and 32 are from *Czech Functionalism 1918–38,* AA Publications, 1987

Contents

Eva Jiricna Architects is an extremely busy practice. At the time of writing it consisted of a staff of thirteen in addition to the principal. No office of this size, and particularly none working such long hours or with such tight deadlines, could possibly operate as a despotism under the control of one individual. Clearly all the work illustrated here is the result of collaboration. Eva Jiricna Architects is a skilled and capable team.

But there are firms of architects where the principal is the beating heart of the enterprise. Like many but not all gifted architects, Eva Jiricna inspires immense personal loyalty in her staff. She too works long hours. She too misses lunch, works through evenings and ignores weekends. All the conversations upon which this book is based were held around a table in the middle of the office, constantly interrupted by the comings and goings of day-to-day business.

If this short book gives the impression that Eva Jiricna Architects consists only of the principal and a number of nameless, faceless assistants, then it is in error. But any approach to the work of this unique architectural practice leads rapidly to the personality and uncompromising opinions of Eva Jiricna herself. Whatever the author's intention, that was what this book ended up being about.

When Will You Join the Party?

Bata store, Prague.
Ludvik Kysela, 1928

"I think you could say that for the Lloyd's building I designed everything that was black." Eva Jiricna, 1990

For an architect best known in Europe and the United States as a designer of high-tech shops with spectacular staircases, Eva Jiricna's own office is a surprising place. It is appropriately sited just off Oxford Street in the West End of London, with its collection of dinosaur department stores and short-lease lock-ups that her retail designing skills have done so much to render obsolete, but it does not look like a ruthless machine for designing in. Eva Jiricna and her staff occupy a charming nineteenth-century baroque house with a steeply pitched roof and bow windows above an empty Michiko boutique that may or may not one day be incorporated into it. The building is easy to miss, but look at it closely and you realise that it is unique in its perfection of type: somewhat more European than English, somewhat more Czechoslovakian than European. When in 1990 Eva Jiricna stood on the rooftop gallery of the town hall in Old Town Square in Prague, during the filming of Gina and Jeremy Newsom's BBC documentary *Closely Observed Buildings*, she gazed down on a roofscape of houses that looked like nothing so much as her own London office a thousand miles away. A building that she leased on the spot one morning in 1985, without having seen inside because the agent had mislaid the keys.

Despite her fairytale London office and romantic Central European origins, Eva Jiricna did not have a romantic childhood. She was born in the Czechoslovakian city of Zlin, the first and nearest approximation to Aldous Huxley's *Brave New World* to be built in the twentieth century. Zlin was a European prototype for the complete Modernist city, of which perhaps the last to be built was Brasilia, half a century later. Zlin was the creation of Tomas Bata, the founder of a famous Czechoslovak industrial dynasty. In the 1920s and 1930s Bata was openly described as the Henry Ford of Czechoslovakia. He was the first to rationalise the production of boots and shoes and turn them into an export commodity for sale all over the world. So great was the expansion of his shoe-manufacturing empire before the Second World War that Bata factory towns were built in England (at East Tilbury), France (at Hellocourt), Germany (at Ottmuth) and in Switzerland, Poland, Hungary, Yugoslavia, Africa, India

Bata mausoleum, Zlin.
Frantisek Gahura, 1937

Bata head office, Zlin.
Vladimir Karfik, 1938

and Canada, where the company headquarters now resides. Tomas Bata died in an air crash in 1937 and a modern mausoleum, with the aircraft in which he was killed suspended from the roof, was built in his memory by the Zlin city architect, Frantisek Gahura. Control of the Bata empire then devolved to his son, Jan, who remained in charge until he finally left Czechoslovakia in 1948. Until then the Batas, father and son, were among the richest and most powerful men in the world.

Like most self-made men, Tomas Bata is remembered for his sayings, one of which was: "I am not rich enough to buy cheap things." It is a statement that Eva Jiricna remembers her father repeating to her, and one that may indeed have some resonance in the later application of her talents to the precise use of high-quality materials in the design of expensive retail shops.

Tomas Bata made Zlin the centre of his operations in the late 1920s and soon turned it into the third centre of Modern architecture in Czechoslovakia, after Prague and Brno. He built factories and housing for workers and within a decade the population had increased from 30,000 to 90,000. He had the centre of the city replanned by Gahura according to a 6 metre grid, vertical as well as horizontal, which meant that every building and street had to conform to an invisible system of regulating lines that governed its length, width and height. The most important building in Zlin, the Bata head office, was a science-fiction, seventeen-storey reinforced concrete tower block designed by the architect Vladimir Karfik and built in 1938. Its elevators and service stairs were outrigged beyond the floor slabs like those of Richard Rogers' Lloyd's building some forty years later. The first skyscraper in Czechoslovakia and one of the first open-plan office buildings in Europe, this structure possessed a novel feature that has never been copied. Jan Bata's own office suite was built into a 36 square metre, glass-sided, air-conditioned elevator equipped with a toilet module, telephones and a Lamson vacuum document communication system. Without leaving his desk, Bata could visit every floor in the building and oversee work at every level.

Another of Tomas Bata's slogans was: "Living separately: working together." To achieve this, Zlin was zoned into separate living and working areas, its residential sections dotted with small brick houses modelled on those of the Garden City movement in England. But at Zlin these houses were not intended to be permanent. They were designed to accustom the thousands of peasant workers drawn from their fields to the new factories to the reality of urban life and work. At the end of ten years, Bata intended to move the occupants on to more advanced residential areas, thus freeing the original houses for the next generation. It was in one of these small dwellings, conceived as a unit of temporary accommodation in a great social and industrial plan, that Eva Jiricna was born.

The new residential areas intended to supplant the brick houses at Zlin were to have taken the form of a development drawn up for Tomas Bata by Le Corbusier following a visit to the city in 1935. Le Corbusier's vision, intended for construction in the 1940s, called for a series of huge concrete superblocks to be distributed over newly laid-out parklands in the Drevnice valley, within easy reach of the Bata factories. Each twelve-storey superblock was to have housed up to 1,600 families, with internal streets at high levels fronted by shops, laundries, schools and crèches. The rooftops were to have featured gardens, playgrounds and sports facilities, including running tracks. In the event these huge structures were never built, though three smaller *Unités d'habitation* of this type were constructed in France by Le Corbusier after the Second World War.

Eva Jiricna's parents moved to Zlin, the Bata company town, in 1938. She was born in one of the small houses built by Bata for his workers, right. The choice of brick was a conscious decision to soften the impact of urban life for new arrivals to the city

Josef Jiricny's promising career in the Bata architects department was cut short by the outbreak of war and Communist seizure of power

It was with this utopian industrial empire, unique in Europe if not the world, that Eva Jiricna's father, Josef Jiricny (in the Czech language male and female names are differentiated by spelling), sought employment in 1938. Josef was the son of a minor official in the Imperial Austro-Hungarian governmental system, a man who once painted a moustache on a portrait of the Emperor Franz Josef to show his Czech patriotism. Born in 1910 in Nova Paka in Bohemia, Josef was unable to choose between a career as an artist or an electrical engineer. In the end he trained as an architect at the Technical University of Prague, though he was to muse over his earlier ambitions from time to time throughout his life. Eva's mother, Eva Svata, was born in Studenec near the Sudetenland in 1911. Her traditionalist parents had refused to let her attend university, though she was allowed to travel to learn languages and in 1933 spent some time at Pitman's College in London. After that she entered the small family business of linen manufacture, working in their retail shop in Prague.

After his graduation in 1935, Josef, like all male Czechoslovakians of his age, was conscripted to serve for two years in the Czechoslovak army, manning the fortifications built to protect the country's fragile western frontier. When he was demobilised in the autumn of 1937 he and Eva Svata were married and went to live in the mining town of Ostrava, where Josef had found work. In the economic circumstances of the time his work was not well paid; in fact he was soon induced by his company to work for nothing until conditions improved. He and Eva were saved from this virtual slavery by her mother, who found a newspaper advertisement for jobs with the Bata architectural department in Zlin and prevailed upon Josef to answer it.

To the family's great relief Josef was shortlisted for a job at Bata. He travelled to Zlin and, at the commencement of his interview with the great Jan Bata, he bowed and introduced himself in the German fashion as "Architect Jiricny". Bata, who manufactured millions of pairs of shoes a year, introduced himself in turn as "Shoemaker Bata".

But just as a generation later Eva Jiricna's architectural career was thrust upon her by the tide of events in modern Czechoslovak history, so was that of her father the victim of similar forces. Josef Jiricny was successful in his application to join the Bata architects department and in

1938 the family moved from penury in Ostrava to relative prosperity in Zlin. But Josef's dreams of designing important functionalist buildings like those of Gahura or Karfik were not to be realised. He had barely begun working in the vast Bata drafting studios when Czechoslovakia was transformed by the consequences of the Munich political settlement. Within a year, the country had been partitioned and Europe was at war.

During the uncertain years of the German ascendancy, Josef Jiricny designed public exhibitions for Bata and entered architectural competitions – "doing and losing" as he ruefully described the process to his daughter years later. Following the German reverses before Moscow in the winter of 1942, the situation of Czechoslovakia worsened. The Bata factories were engaged in war production and in 1943 Zlin began to suffer bombing attacks. In the autumn of 1943 Eva remembers the entire population of her nursery school being marched out of the town into the surrounding woods, there to watch as the Soviet bombers smashed the heart of the Bata industrial complex, leaving the city shrouded in smoke for days. In the winter of 1945 the architects department was finally moved out of the city and the Jiricna household accommodated in a country house on the outskirts of Prague belonging to one of the Bata directors. There Eva's father was put to work on ambitious plans for the post-war reconstruction of Zlin. But as the German retreat turned into a rout, the advancing Soviet forces encircled Prague, destroying everything in their path. The Bata country house was requisitioned and turned into a military hospital. The occupants were driven out and the plans for a new Zlin, along with all the "bourgeois" furniture in the building, were burned in a vast conflagration in the grounds.

Refugees in their own country, for the three years following the war Eva and her father and mother lived with her paternal grandfather in a small and overcrowded house in the centre of Prague. Eva recalls that one of her grandfather's sayings was: "In life you always get what you want, but too much of it and much too late." But it is perhaps a better measure of those traumatic years that she remained an only child until 1948, when her sister Vera was born. Her brother Josef was not born until 1951.

After the Communist seizure of power in 1948, the Bata empire was taken over by the state and Jan Bata fled to Canada. The city of Zlin was renamed Gottwaldov in honour of the Czech Communist leader. In that year Josef, still an employee of the company, was dismissed by the new Communist management. He steadfastly refused to join the Communist Party and in an increasingly regimented society this refusal to conform was an intermittent career liability. From 1948 he remained an employee of the State Architects Bureau, the central employment agency for all architects. But his early expertise with exhibitions was not forgotten and in 1956 he was commissioned to design large trade exhibitions in China, Moscow and other parts of Europe. He also worked on the Czechoslovak pavilion at the Brussels World Exhibition of 1958 but was subsequently placed in an insignificant research unit at the Bureau, where he remained until the beginning of the liberalisation of the Dubcek era. Then in 1968, only months before Soviet opposition to the Dubcek reforms culminated in the reoccupation of Prague by the Red Army, he was made project architect for the much admired Czechoslovak pavilion at the Osaka World Exposition of 1970 and spent two years in Japan supervising its construction. On his return journey he had intended to travel to London to visit his children, but by an agreement between the participating governments, all Czech nationals admitted to Japan in connection with Expo '70 were permitted to leave only on flights passing through Moscow. In the autumn of 1970 Josef Jiricny returned to Czechoslovakia and very soon afterwards fell ill. A mishandled gall-bladder operation led to post-operative infection and after a long illness he died in 1972. By then an emigré herself, Eva was not permitted to re-enter the country to see him before he died.

The chequered career of Josef Jiricny under Communist rule in Czechoslovakia was to have unexpected consequences for his daughter. Her life until the age of nine had been characterised by a series of terrifying changes played out against the background of the greatest European conflagration of modern times. When she first attended school, German was a compulsory language, then the school system broke down completely, and then Russian took the place of German. At the age of ten she was the only girl in her class of thirty who was not a member of the Young Pioneers, the Communist youth organisation, because her father would not permit it. She threw herself into her studies and by the early age of twelve was sure that her vocation was to be a research chemist.

When Will You Join the Party?

Year after year she excelled at chemistry until in 1956, her final year at high school, a new chemistry teacher committed to the principles of socialist realism in education set as a compulsory examination question the task of explaining how an iron foundry worked. Eva had never been interested in those areas outside the ambit of pure chemistry; for the first time in her life she failed to gain top marks.

Eva remembers this incident as a crushing blow. But after a period of some confusion, she soon came to believe that her father's profession, architecture, might make an acceptable substitute. Josef was not encouraging: "Women architects are hopeless," was his opinion. He thought there might be more possibilities in interior design or fashion. However, as is often the case, parental opposition only served to re-inforce his daughter's at first uncertain preference. Adequately qualified in all but drawing skills, she entered the Technical University of Prague in 1956 as a first-year architecture student. She pursued the course there uninterrupted for six years, graduating in 1962.

At a distance of thirty years, Eva's recollections of the training that was to play such a crucial part in her life are not sharp. Her professors – in many cases the instigators of the revolutionary, avant-garde architecture of the pre-war period in Czechoslovakia, now termed by the Communists the "bourgeois republic" – were afraid to discuss it. Instead

Student projects for a housing estate and a nursery school, right, reinforced the idea that the most important task for the new generation of architects working under socialism was the rebuilding of the country

she and her fellow students were taught that it had been a creative impulse robbed of social value by capitalistic market forces. The great tasks confronting their generation, they were told, were not stylistic or aesthetic but social and industrial: the rebuilding of the country; the housing of the masses; the creation of a socialist state.

Of the six years of an arduous training that comprised more science and engineering than would have been the case in Britain, Eva remembers most clearly the unrelenting seriousness of her professors. From the very first they stressed the privileged status of the architect and his or her responsibility for the quality of life and its physical survival in the buildings they designed. It is perhaps the only moral aspect of her training in Czechoslovakia that to this day she believes was correct and of value.

When Eva Jiricna graduated at the age of twenty-three, she entered the workforce of an impoverished socialist society, not a rich economy of capitalist opportunity. There was no question of her being free to seek a position where she wished; a faculty job placement committee, consisting of professors, Communist Party members and student representatives, decided where every graduate should work for their first three years. In Eva's case, the question was complicated by an earlier exchange with the head of the department, a professor of urban planning and the senior Communist representative in the faculty. At the beginning of her final year, he had summoned her to his office and asked her a loaded question:

"When would you like to join the Party?"

"Which one?" she answered without thinking.

The professor was shocked. "The Communist Party, of course," he replied. Eva answered that she did not wish to join the Communist Party and the interview came to an end.

Perhaps as a consequence of this exchange, Eva found herself invited in the summer of 1962 to report to a cement factory in the rough mining town of Kladno. When she arrived for her interview, the director stared at her and announced: "I don't want any women here. A woman like you will make the men restless and reduce production." Eva was not allowed to use the men's accommodation at the mine and so had to leave Prague at 5.00am each day in order to report to work at 7.30. She soon fell ill and was released for medical reasons.

Eva Jiricna graduated from Prague Technical University in 1962

The second task found for her by the State Architects Bureau turned out to be surprisingly congenial. Eva was seconded to the Ministry of Education and sent to teach foreign students at the University of 17 November, a chaotic Marxist institution filled with students from all over the Third World. The official teaching language was Czech, but a riot of languages was spoken. Eva taught architecture there for two years, during which time she learned French and English. She also took a masters degree in architecture at night school and began to enter design competitions on her own account.

In 1963 she met and married a Czech architect named Martin Holub and, typically in the cramped post-war conditions, the couple shared a flat with Holub's mother. It was the first time that Eva, reared against a background of spartan Czech functionalist interiors, had ever encountered so-called antique furniture and kitsch interior decoration. Even now she remembers how much she hated her mother-in-law's apartment. "How could anyone live with such old rubbish, sofas and chairs, wall-hangings, *House and Garden*... It was only many years later that I came to understand that genuine antiques had some of the same qualities as the modern furniture that I knew and loved."

Although Eva's marriage to Holub did not finally end in divorce until 1973, the couple separated after only three years. Eva meanwhile secured a job at the Czech Institute of Fashion and Industrial Design and in 1965 was introduced to foreign travel when she was invited by the Union Internationale des Architectes (UIA) to attend its Paris congress, on the strength of a winning entry to a furniture design competition. The experience was to change her life. As an attractive young woman of twenty-six and a capable linguist, she gained entrance to every major social event of the congress, propelled into the company of such international figures as the engineer Félix Candela, and Oscar Niemeyer, architect of the great new capital city of Brazil. But after two weeks of this joyous freedom she was compelled to return to the unsuccessful marriage, the shared flat and the bureaucratic institute in Prague where she was engaged in design studies for a textile factory that would never be built. "At that moment of return," she recalls, "I would have accepted any offer to go anywhere as long as it was beyond the iron curtain."

Another opportunity arose with the holding of the next UIA congress in Prague in 1967. On this occasion Eva found herself a guide for many of the visiting architects from the West. Among others she showed the city to two architects from London, Ernö Goldfinger and Jack Whittle, the latter at that time deputy chief architect at the Greater London Council (GLC). It was Whittle who by painstaking work over the next year arranged the work permit that enabled her to leave Prague on 31 July 1968 to fly to London for what was intended as a six-month secondment to the schools division of the GLC architects department.

Less than a month after Eva arrived in London, Soviet tanks clattered through the streets of Prague and the Dubcek administration was over-thrown. Thousands of people fled across the border to Austria, many making their way to London. There could be no question of Eva returning now. She was already living in the land of *Sergeant Pepper*, Stop the Shop, the Drugstore and Carnaby Street. Her decision to remain against the terms of her government exit permit was like being released from a prison but never being allowed to go back to it. She was in fact sentenced to three years imprisonment *in absentia* for the offence by a Prague court. Eva paid a high price for her freedom. The last time she saw her father was when he kissed her goodbye at the airport five years before he died. In 1976 she became a British citizen. She was not to return to Czechoslovakia for twenty-two years.

The GLC architects department proved to be something of a disap-pointment. As Eva remembers it, the chief creative activity was contriving to appear busy, even though there was no apparent difference in the state of affairs at the end of a week or a month, whether any work had been done or not. Obvious relief from the tedium of the glacial progress of drawings across the drawing board, such as might have been gained from a visit to the library, was forbidden except on the express instruction of a section leader. But this was Swinging London of the 1960s. The hours at the GLC were short and there was freedom to enjoy. Freedom: a concept that persons who grew up in Eastern Europe can never adequately explain to those who grew up in Western Europe. Even today Eva stumbles over her words as she tries to describe it. "You people here can go anywhere and say anything. You can fly to New York or Paris. You can open a market stall to sell vegetables without being sent to prison. You can study architecture not agriculture, if that's your wish. You can leave your job and find another. When I arrived here I was astonished at how much freedom there is, and I still am."

After a year of inertia at the GLC, Eva left the public sector for the private and applied for a job with the firm of Louis de Soissons to work on the Brighton Marina. Working on a coastal project appealed to her, she says, because Czechoslovakia has no sea. Besides, the immense £140 million project for a yacht harbour and marina, hotels and housing on reclaimed land – still uncompleted in the form proposed by the architects on the day it was opened by the Queen in 1978 – called for considerable feats of engineering design. From 1969 until 1978, through the vicissitudes of a 1973 public inquiry, the Arab oil embargo and the energy crisis that followed it, the three-day week and the great inflation, Eva worked for Louis de Soissons and the Brighton Marina Company, at first commuting from a bedsitter in Tonbridge Wells and later from Central London. She rose through the organisation and eventually became project architect.

As she sees those years now, Brighton Marina taught her two important things. Because of the heavy engineering component of the scheme, she learned the value of simplification. "None of the main elements was cheap, and every unnecessary one cost at least a million pounds." She also learned about the performance of materials in a severe environment. Even though little that she designed was built, from the world of yachts, boats, ships, harbours, storms and breakwaters she took many lessons that were to stand her in good stead later on. She learned that stainless steel is not rustproof; that round portholes have no leak-points; that tensile cable structures can withstand incredible loads; that high-tech materials such as steel, aluminium, glass fibre, neoprene, composites and laminates can only justify their cost when expertly designed and conscientiously installed. "All the materials I have ever used in the shops, staircases and apartments I have designed since, I learned about at Brighton Marina," said Eva years afterwards. And the statement is very nearly true.

For most of the time she worked on Brighton Marina, Eva was living with Jan Kaplicky, a fellow Czech whom she had known slightly in Prague. Kaplicky arrived in London after the Soviet invasion of 1968 and worked initially for Sir Denys Lasdun. In 1971 he joined Richard Rogers

Once she had moved to Britain, Louis de Soissons' £140 million project for hotels, housing and a yacht harbour at Brighton Marina occupied Eva Jiricna for ten years

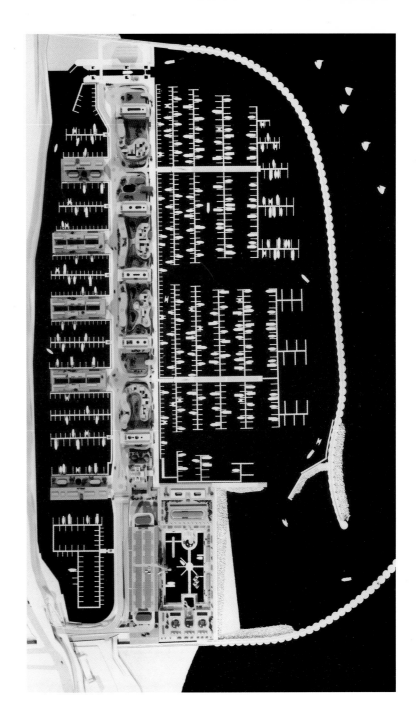

When Will You Join the Party?

and Partners and was one of the team that, together with Renzo Piano, won the Paris competition for the design of the Centre Pompidou. He later worked for two years on the Marina and then taught at the Architectural Association and worked for Foster Associates. In 1979 he founded his own practice, Future Systems, specialising in advanced technology architectural projects including research work for NASA.

Indirectly it was through her association with Jan Kaplicky that Eva's career as an independent architect began. In 1978 she had left the Louis de Soissons office with the partner in charge of the Marina project, David Hodges, who had resigned over disagreements with the Brighton Marina Company. She continued to work with Hodges until 1982 on a number of feasibility studies and competitions, which they entered using the name Hodges Jiricna Partnership. They were working on their winning entry for the Westminster Pier competition – a project that was abruptly abandoned two years later without fees or compensation – at the same time as Jan Kaplicky was assigned by Norman Foster to work on the design of a shop in Sloane Street for an impulsive Moroccan-born designer and retail genius named Joseph Ettedgui. Eva went with Jan to the opening of the shop and met Coco, Joseph's wife. Her first Ettedgui job was for her, moving a partition between two children's bedrooms and designing some furniture. But in due course Joseph himself took an interest. One day he telephoned her at the offices of Hodges Jiricna.

Though little of what she designed was ever built, Brighton Marina gave Eva Jiricna valuable experience in the use of high-tech materials and techniques

"I have a little shop in South Molton Street," he said. "I want it to be designed like the Norman Foster Sloane Street shop but much cheaper and much quicker."

That little shop in South Molton Street, which still exists, set the career of Eva Jiricna architect upon a new course. It was published in *Design* magazine and became a critical success. Subsequently Joseph asked her to redesign his apartment. That job was also published and then followed Le Caprice restaurant, another Joseph shop, a shop for Kenzo and eventually a steady stream of commissions. From 1982 to 1984 Eva worked independently in the office of Richard Rogers, who hoped that she could win the commission to design the interior of the Lloyd's building. But except for the design of the restaurant and some key fixtures and fittings which betray her expert touch, this ambitious project ended in disappointment. Instead in 1984, with a substantial commission to redesign one floor of Harrods department store in Knightsbridge as the Way-In boutique, where the design work was shared with Future Systems, Eva Jiricna set up her own practice, Jiricna Kerr Associates, with the designer Kathy Kerr. The firm prospered but the partnership was not successful and in 1985 Kathy Kerr left for the United States. In 1986 the practice was renamed Eva Jiricna Architects and Eva took over the lease on the house over the shop in Dering Street that has been her office ever since.

The heavy engineering component of the Marina project was an important lesson in the value of simplification

When Will You Join the Party?

On Living in a Young Country

"The artists of the Empire of Utopia had a decided preference for the art forms of past epochs. They reconstructed ancient cities in such a way that one could believe oneself to be living in remote antiquity. Many Utopians began to inhabit these ancient cities, wearing the costume of old days and imitating the customs of that time as faithfully as possible.

"This fashion trend favouring the ancient had, however, provoked a counter movement, and thus there were many painters, sculptors and especially architects who were possessed by the keen desire to live in the future." Paul Scheerbart, *The Emperor of Utopia*, 1904

The day Eva Jiricna was born in the city of Zlin, the republic of Czechoslovakia had twelve more days to live. On 15 March 1939 Hitler's armies crossed the frontier from Austria unopposed and occupied Prague. The government fled, the country was partitioned, and Bohemia and Moravia were absorbed into the Third Reich. As with all Czechoslovakians born in the twentieth century, the story of Eva Jiricna's life is bound up with the remarkable, tragic and brilliant history of her country. So too is the derivation of her genius as a designer and architect.

The origins of Czech functionalism are nowhere well understood. Superficially this art and architecture could be seen as only one of a number of national expressions of the internationalist ideas of the Modern avant-garde in the years after the First World War; in fact its roots penetrate much deeper into Czech history and conventional wisdom leaves important questions unanswered. Why, for instance, did Modernism in Czechoslovakia become the national architecture of a non-Communist bourgeois state? Why was there no reflection in Czech culture of the resurgent neoclassicism and sentimental folkish vernacular that swept through the rest of Europe in the 1930s? The true answers to these questions cannot be found in the short and tragic history of the Czech republic of 1918, but must be sought in the character of the Czech people and the role of their country during the previous Austrian ascendancy. Czechoslovakia is a country that has repeatedly suddenly achieved independence, and just as suddenly lost it.

The republic of Czechoslovakia that exists today is a small country that was once a great kingdom. In the thirteenth century its capital city, Prague, was the seat of the rulers of Bohemia, a kingdom reaching from the Baltic to the Adriatic Sea. But in 1530 the Bohemian crown fell to Austria by marriage and in the ensuing conflict between Protestant and Catholic the country was torn to pieces by the divisions of the Reformation. In a pattern that was to recur in the modern history of Czechoslovakia, when the Protestant Bohemians finally rose against Austria and elected their own king, Frederick V, son-in-law of James I of England, their independence was brief. At the Battle of the White Mountain in 1620 Frederick was defeated and Protestantism forbidden.

During the "300 years of Austrian subjection" that followed, the present-day boundaries of Czechoslovakia enclosed two provinces of the kingdom of Austria – Bohemia and Moravia – which were ruled from Vienna by way of a provincial governor in Prague. By the end of the nineteenth century, when Austria and Hungary had merged into an empire second in size only to Imperial Russia, much of Bohemia and Moravia was occupied by vast hunting estates belonging to the imperial nobility.

But in the latter years of the Austro-Hungarian empire not all of Bohemia and Moravia was feudal. Like all of Europe, the empire had industrialised and, having industrialised before electrification, its industries had grown up where its raw materials were. The empire's richest coalfields and largest mineral reserves – iron, gold, copper, lead, zinc and nickel – were found in the provinces of Bohemia and Moravia and by 1918 no less than 75 per cent of the manufacturing industry of all Austro-Hungary was concentrated in this area. Even sixty-six years later, the People's Republic of Czechoslovakia, the ninety-second largest country in the world and a centrally planned, inefficient Communist economy, still ranked eleventh in terms of industrial output.

When freedom finally came with the defeat of Austro-Hungary in 1918, Czech architecture drew from a strong industrial base of natural resources, scientific and technical skills, and a technical education system that could match any in the world. It was this power that underlay the often-quoted independence day promise of architect Jan Kotera: "We will catch and overtake all Europe."

Advanced technology architecture can only flourish where there is industry to support its demand for refined materials and precision components. In Czechoslovakia this resource existed in the old imperial munitions industry. As early as 1880 the Steyr armaments company of

The fledgling Czech democracy was an important industrial centre between the two world wars. Its armaments firms are still famous, but the Czech aviation and motor industries, once pace-setters with designs such as the A-204 transport plane of 1936 and Tatra limousine of 1933, below, have wasted away

Moravia was the largest producer of small arms in the world. In 1893 Steyr marketed the world's first automatic pistol and seventy years later the country was still the source of the world's most advanced plastic explosives. This industry was the seed from which Czechoslovak manufacturing grew in the 1920s and 1930s. The largest and most advanced concern was the Skoda munitions group of Pilsen, Western Bohemia, which had started life as an ironworks in 1886. After 1914 Skoda was joined by the Prague engine company Praga and then by the vehicle producer Tatra. Two of the most important automobile engineers of the twentieth century – Ferdinand Porsche and Hans Ledwinka – emerged from this background, although neither adopted Czech nationality.

It is a matter of history that the architecture of the new Czechoslovakian republic followed the same path of innovative engineering as its motor industry. But unlike Porsche and Ledwinka, the Czech functionalist architects Havlicek and Honzik, Fragner, Bens, Krejcar, Fuchs and Zak had to confront an inevitable cultural bias in favour of the old and the familiar. Motor vehicles were expendable; they were expected to pursue a process of continual development with each successive model demonstrably better and more reliable than its predecessor. Buildings, on the other hand, were cultural objects in the public domain, part of the historic environment that established the national identity.

The manner in which the Czech functionalist architects were able to evade opposition to their work from the kind of hostility that was to crush Modern architecture in Germany and the Soviet Union was almost unique. Czechoslovakia rejected its architectural heritage in favour of the challenge of the new because this very heritage was a foreign imposition. In a remarkable parallel with Ireland, a country that gained independence at almost the same time, Czechoslovakia rejected 300 years of Viennese classical and revivalist architecture as a legacy of colonialism. We can see how this process worked by analogy with Ireland.

In the Ireland of today there is no Heritage Fund, no Civic Trust, no Royal Fine Art Commission, no National Trust, no Historic Buildings Council. The buildings of the old English ascendancy that are carefully preserved can be counted on the fingers of one hand and all of them are structures that played a historic part in the achievement of Irish independence, like the Dublin central Post Office besieged by the British army in

Adolf Bens, designer of pavilions for the Paris 1925 and Liège 1931 exhibitions, and Bohuslav Fuchs, who worked in Brno

1916. In the Republic of Ireland the indigenous Georgian architecture is not seen as a rich heritage, but as the most prominent evidence of the "Protestant ascendancy", the hated era of English colonial rule that ended with the creation of the Irish Free State. And in the newly independent Czechoslovakian republic, the classical, baroque, aristocratic heritage of Austrian rule was seen in precisely the same way.

If there was a Czech architecture before the "Austrian ascendancy", it consisted of Bohemian castles set among mountain forests, peasant villages and medieval towns. By the 1920s it had attained the mythological status of the Celtic, pre-occupation architecture of Ireland. In reality, throughout the 300 years of Austrian rule, the architecture of Prague and the other Czechoslovak towns and cities came to echo that of Vienna, as that of Dublin did London. Palaces, theatres and apartment houses were built on the imperial model. Renaissance and baroque fronts transformed the appearance of the stone and timber buildings of the medieval city centre, then classical and gothic fronts recovered those. And finally the avant-garde art and architectural movements of the *fin-de-siècle* period – the Vienna Secession, Art Nouveau and even Cubism – one by one left their mark.

In the Austrian empire, as in the rest of Europe, Modernism was no more than an artistic and intellectual game until the bloodbath of the First World War. The archetypal pre-war Modernist was an effete artist; the archetypal post-war Modernist a "New Man" – a soldier returning brutalised from the Front with the determination to build a new society. It was this "New Man" who ruled the architectural avant-garde of Europe for two decades after 1918, and in Czechoslovakia most of all, where the need for a national identity and the existence of a high-tech industrial base gave him the means to realise his vision of a functional utopia on an unprecedented scale.

The "New Men" of Modernism believed that, because of industrialisation, the creation of all works of art, including architecture, should be no different from the process of industrial design for mass production. No different in its way from the publishing of newspapers, or the making of films, typewriters, cars or aeroplanes. All such man-made things in an industrial age should, they said, be viewed as useful instruments, not fine-art monuments. Functionalism was the name given to the pursuit of

Karel Teige, leader of the Constructivist group, Devetsil, invited international Modern Movement architects to Czechoslovakia

Department store, Ostrava. Erich Mendelsohn, 1932 Bottom: Tugendhat house, Brno. Mies van der Rohe, 1930

this Modern doctrine of usefulness. According to its principles, the quality of all the tools of Modern society was henceforth to be assessed, not by the scarcity or material value of these tools, but by the economy of means with which they did their job. In architecture one immediate impact was the disappearance of any requirement for ornament because it made no functional contribution to performance.

In the years following independence, Czechoslovakia increased its exports of manufactured goods and made trade agreements all over Europe. The country exported small arms, guns, tanks and trucks, building components, engines, cars, generators, motor-cycles, aeroplanes, mass-produced shoes and wooden furniture. In addition to money and raw materials, she received from her neighbours all over Europe the revolutionary post-war idea of a machine art and a machine architecture.

The radical artist Karel Teige, leader of the Constructivist group Devetsil, was an important figure in this connection. He met and learned from Auguste Perret and Le Corbusier in Paris; met Adolf Behne in Berlin and Hannes Meyer at the Bauhaus, where he also taught. He invited the many pioneer Modern architects to lecture and teach in Prague, including Adolf Loos, Walter Gropius, Mies van der Rohe, Erich Mendelsohn and J.J.P. Oud. Later these architects returned to contribute individual buildings in Czechoslovakia and to demonstrate their methods at Modern housing projects like Novy Dum, Baba and Zlin.

Adolf Loos, the son of stonemason, was born in 1870 in what was to become one of the Czechoslovak centres of Modern architecture, the city of Brno. A pioneer Modernist much influenced by visits to the United States, he opposed the extravagant decoration of the Secession school then fashionable in Vienna, where he practised. In 1928 Loos came to Prague to design the Villa Muller, a massive, solid-looking concrete building whose interior none the less showed a great liberation of space.

The Villa Muller is a transitional object in many ways. It is artless externally and its interior is inexcusably ponderous, but most revealingly its perfectly preserved interior is finished using expensive materials like marble, wood and glass in a restrained and under-decorated way. This penchant both betrays its Viennese ancestry and establishes it as a prototype for the luxurious Modern architecture of Mies van der Rohe and, half a century later, the shops and restaurants of Eva Jiricna.

The Villa Muller in Prague by Adolf Loos, 1928, combines luxurious materials with a Modernist plan

The Villa Cenek and Villa Heraina by Ladislav Zak, 1933, were among thirty demonstration houses built by functionalist architects in the Prague suburb of Baba

Julis Hotel by the architect Pavel Janak, a Modern building dating from 1932, shows the new Czech architecture in a more fully developed form. Designed as a café, cinema and hotel in the commercial centre of Wenceslas Square, Julis is a flat-roofed, open-planned multi-storey concrete frame structure with a steel framed curtain wall elevation to the front. This facade consists almost entirely of glass because it carries no weight. Such an "open" elevation would have been impossible without the example of Le Corbusier; it would also have been impossible without Czechoslovakia's capacity for precision manufacture in steel and glass.

In 1933 a demonstration project of thirty functionalist houses and apartments was built in the Prague suburb of Baba to explore the possibilities of Modern single-family housing developments built on a large scale. Virtually all the Czech functionalist architects of note contributed designs and even today, in their much deteriorated condition, the remaining villas convey the enormous liberation of the functionalist ideal from the historicist past, with their roof-terraces, cantilevered balconies, external staircases and "as few useless objects and as much cleanness and whiteness as possible," as the architect Jan Koula insisted.

The Villa Fric by architect Ladislav Zak, completed in 1935, demonstrates to perfection the Czech functionalist ideal of open planning and the interpenetration of interior and exterior space. Not a low-cost housing unit but an expensive house in a Prague suburb, this reinforced concrete building reverses the traditional order of floors with an interconnected roof garden, living room and study above bedrooms and ancillary accommodation. Because it has been preserved almost unchanged for more than fifty years, this high-level complex uniquely demonstrates how the austere means of the functionalist school could none the less achieve luxury in the use of space. The house today still conveys the stark emptiness, light and clarity of form that was the postwar reaction against the ornamental excesses of the Vienna school.

But brilliantly successful though its art, architecture and industry were, the fact remained that the state of Czechoslovakia had been created as an instrument of policy by the winning side in a war that had not been its own war of liberation. The country had risen almost accidentally from the ashes of one empire and was soon to be destroyed by the growth of another. Its frontiers, confirmed by the Peace Treaty of

On Living in a Young Country

The Villa Fric in Prague, designed in 1935 by leading Czech functionalist architect Ladislav Zak, above

Saint-Germain-en-Laye in 1920, enclosed a heterogeneous population of 14 million made up of only 7 million Czechs in Bohemia and Moravia, plus 3 million Germans in the Sudetenland, 2 million Slovaks and vocal Hungarian and Romanian minorities as well.

It was the creation of Nazi Germany in 1933 that first began to threaten the stability of this combination. Elements among the Sudeten Germans had long wished to secede to Austria, but it was not until March 1938, with the unification of Germany and Austria, that the new German Reich began to offer active support to their cause. In May 1938 tensions between Germany and Czechoslovakia reached such a pitch that the Czechs prepared for war. With only nominal support from France or the Soviet Union, Czechoslovakia could have repulsed Hitler at that time. But after months of uncertainty the British and French premiers met the Axis powers at Munich and issued a joint call for the ceding of Sudetenland to Germany. Robbed of its defensible western frontier, the rump of Czechoslovakia could not long survive. The German invasion of 1939 led to the incorporation of the old Austrian provinces of Bohemia and Moravia into the Reich as the Protectorate of Bohemia and Moravia. Other parts of the country were handed over to Hungary and Poland. Slovakia was allowed to form a Slovak Free State, closely allied to Germany.

From then on the fortunes of the country followed the initial success and later disastrous failure of Nazi Germany's invasion of Soviet Russia. Against this background the eclipse of Czech Modern architecture assumed trivial proportions. It was not until January 1945 that a Czechoslovak government in exile was able to return to the country under the protection of the Red Army. After the surrender of the German forces in Prague to the Soviet and United States armies in May, a National Front provisional government was proclaimed, with the Communists led by Klement Gottwald now the largest party. In the first post-war general election of May 1946 only National Front parties were eligible and voting was compulsory. The Communists won a huge majority. In 1948 the Communists seized absolute power and a second general election was held with no opposition list. An 89 per cent vote for the Communist Party was recorded and President Benes, the last survivor of the pre-war government, resigned. Klement Gottwald became president and ushered in forty years of Communist rule broken only by the Prague Spring of 1968.

The post-war reconstruction of the republic followed collectivist lines. Like other professionals, all architects became employees of the state, their labour directed to whichever sector of the economy was deemed to be most in need of their services. Where pre-war Czech functionalist design had been an expression of the primacy of free-market economics, the free movement of capital across national boundaries and rising private wealth, post-war Czech Modernism was entirely at the mercy of the strengths and weaknesses of a planned economy.

The "bourgeois individualism" that had produced the brilliantly advanced private villas and housing estates of the period 1925–38 had been killed off by the war and the death or emigration of many of the talented architects responsible. For those who remained, the exigencies of the new economy required that heavy concrete construction replace steel and the needs of industry and the labour force assumed the highest priority. In the interest of high-density development served by public transport, high-rise housing replaced single-family detached units. As in the Soviet Union and other Eastern bloc satellites, prefabricated panel-lised housing systems dominated the housing industry. With an unconvertible currency, there was now no two-way traffic in ideas with Western Europe. Foreign architectural and design magazines and books were virtually unobtainable. Under state control, the industrial giants of the pre-war era – Skoda, CKD, Tatra, Praga – still existed and still exported on a large scale, but their quality declined. Where in the years of the "bourgeois Republic" Czechoslovakian consumer products had led the world, in the years of the "People's Republic" they slipped into a back-water of obsolescence, competing only through artificially low pricing.

But despite this general decline, Czech architecture during the Soviet ascendancy never ceased to be Modern. Industrial architects in particular strove to be well informed of developments all over the world and remained competitive in their design skills. As in other socialist countries, industrial architecture held an aesthetic status under the Czechoslovak planned economy that it has never held in the West. It was principally in the cultural sphere, when massive works of architecture were attempted, that the effort to match the achievements of the pre-war republic most clearly failed. The vast urban planning and design concept of the Klement Gottwald bridge and the Palace of Culture in Prague, completed in 1981, exemplify the new weakness of inspiration and technical backwardness.

Yet while the post-war planned economy explicitly acknowledged a debt to the traditions of Czech functionalism, the tradition was modified in accordance with the country's subordination to the more reactionary Soviet Union. A Stalinist building like the Hotel International built in Prague in 1954, topped by its Red Star and laid out in wedding cake tiers of Moscow-style decoration, perfectly expresses one form this reorientation took. The building's crudely imposing exterior expresses an image of ornate authority, but its interior is dominated by a social realist decorative theme in the form of friezes showing Stakhanovite workers slaving at the tasks of the economy.

Another aspect of this reorientation is captured by the housing built in the Prague district of Northern Town, visible from the model functionalist villas of Baba. In Northern Town socialist land-use is clearly displayed in the coupling of high-density apartment housing with an extravagant use of open space and no attention to landscaping or detail. Housing more than 100,000 people, Northern Town was assembled using a prefabricated panellised concrete system developed in Czechoslovakia and used in the construction of more than 2 million homes since 1948. While this policy of productivity without variation achieved quantitative successes – so high was the output of panels that by 1985 more than 60 per cent of all the housing in the country had been built since the war at a rate of construction four times higher than that in Britain – it sacrificed popular enthusiasm and support. Economic goals such as that of a massive reduction in the number of person-hours required for the construction of standardised building types did not contribute to the popularity of the Communist regime. In 1950 it required 2,500 hours of labour to complete one apartment; by 1985 the housing industry could complete each apartment in only 500 hours. Not only that, but in its later forms the type of system-building employed was modified to enable the interior fixtures and fittings of the apartments to be refurbished every twenty-five years while the "support structures" themselves lasted for 125 years.

It is the aesthetic and environmental poverty of this collective approach to housing and urbanism that bred much of the opposition to the Communist regime that fell in 1989. Recognisable in its way as a descendant of the aesthetic ruthlessness of the inter-war functionalist period, post-war Czech housing was none the less carried out on such a massive, uniform and insensitive scale that it bred a new resentment against Modernism and a longing for the ancient and individual forms of village life. The rebirth of historicism and the first revolt against the new since 1920 was born in the concrete ghetto of Northern Town.

It is the strength of this reaction that has created the true crisis of Czechoslovakian architecture today. A way forward exists through high-tech design – a genre with expatriate practitioners of the first importance – but the rise of a new capitalistic touristic nostalgia in Prague shows that a way backwards exists too, perhaps for the first time in seventy years.

Old Town Square in Prague epitomises the present crisis. The gothic revival town hall was destroyed in the fighting at the end of the war and an area of grass left in its place. For decades this space was a subject of controversy. In the Communist years repeated architectural competitions were held, all producing Modern solutions, but nothing was built.

In 1990, a year after the country's third escape from imperial domination in seventy years, a public opinion survey determined that what will replace the old town hall will be a faithful reconstruction. This survey was taken when Eva Jiricna had returned to Prague for the first time after an absence of twenty-two years. She visited the town hall site in connection with the BBC documentary *Closely Observed Buildings* and was filmed discussing the question of the old town hall with a crowd of people there. It was a sobering moment. Everyone she spoke to begged her not to support what they called the ruin of the square by the construction of a Modern building. Eva had left her country to escape regimentation and aesthetic censorship, and now here it was resurgent. This episode taught her that the relationship between political history and architecture in Czechoslovakia, once so conducive to a radical Modernism, had turned full circle.

"What the country needs," she wrote on her return, "is the past, the present and the future; and the people who are going to create the future will have to study, travel, read, and visit people who are involved with the present rather than the past. The Czechs have had to wait a long time for their new opportunity. Now they must be allowed to start on a clean page. They are quite capable of battling it out without outside intervention."

Whether to rebuild bombed sites such as Old Town Square in Prague with replicas of the gothic buildings that once occupied them or to start from scratch is a sensitive issue. Vaclav Havel's Czechoslovakia still has to make up its mind whether it sees itself as the heir to the Modernism of the 1920s, or condemns it along with the shoe-box concrete Stalinism

Architecture 1980 1990

Joseph Ettedgui's
Sloane Street
apartment was a small
studio in which sliding
doors and mirrors were
used to make the most
of the limited space.
The apparently
industrial precision
of the doors relied
on Eva Jiricna's close
collaboration with
the craftsmen who
constructed them
using techniques
learned on the
Brighton Marina
project

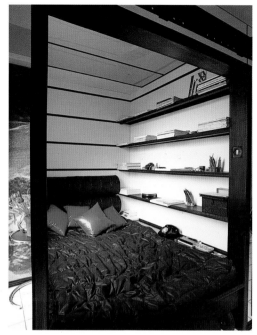

For her own low-budget Belsize Park apartment, Eva Jiricna covered the kitchen in off-cuts from the vibrant green industrial rubber flooring of Norman Foster's Willis Faber Dumas building, right. Sleeping and working were both accommodated in the same area, below, with the bed placed above the plan chest

Wood is not a material with which Eva Jiricna had much experience, but it forms part of the Kenzo house style. For the company's Sloane Street store, she created a sinuous timber stairway with the curves of a grand piano, opposite

This Joseph shop branched out of fashion and into furniture, with Mallet-Stevens chairs on sale upstairs and in use in L'Express café downstairs, right. The glass units on the display wall, opposite, were off-the-peg cladding units put to work in a new context

Working with Jan
Kaplicky's Future
Systems, Jiricna
Architects gutted the
old Way-In, Harrods'
high-fashion floor since
the 1960s, and gave
it a glamorous new
look. The theme was
flexibility, with display
stands on wheels and
stock rooms behind
movable screens

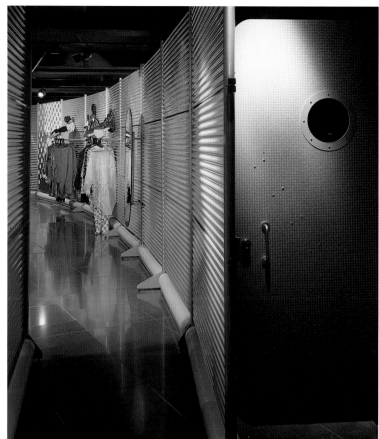

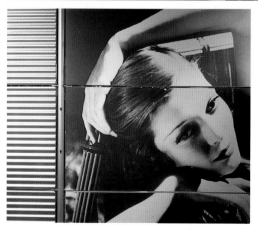

Twin sets of curvaceous, metal-faced steps give the shop the air of a grand entrance. The tortuous geometry of the stair rails as they double back to lead the customer downstairs, opposite, picks up on the same theme

After designing
Le Caprice in 1980,
this was Eva Jiricna's
second attempt at a
restaurant for Joseph
Ettedgui. The space
has a narrow street
frontage occupied by a
bar, below, with a wider
two-level space at the
rear, opposite, where
undulating walls are
offset by the intricate
web of cables that
forms a balustrade

Situated close to
Piccadilly, Legends is a
restaurant by day and
a nightclub after dark.
The undulating ceiling
is defined by extruded
aluminium rods, below,
while the staircase
takes on a baroque
flamboyance, opposite.
It is both a centrepiece
and a platform to see
from and be seen on

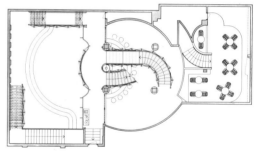

For Vidal Sassoon
in Frankfurt, the
traditional layout of
a hairdressing salon,
with its single row of
chairs and basins, was
reworked in a zig-zag
configuration to offer
more storage space
and privacy

The US company Joan & David commissioned a worldwide chain of shoe shops in 1987. Unlike most of the shops, which are in malls or department stores, the San Francisco branch in Union Square has a real street presence

The central feature of the Joan & David store in Los Angeles' South Coast Plaza, Costa Mesa, is the staircase, with its zig-zag balustrades and glass treads, below. The curved metal that runs around the store at ceiling height, right, is Art Deco in feel

The Joan & David
Faubourg Saint-Honoré
store, a tiny shoebox
of a space with little
room for flamboyance,
relies for its impact
on the polish of its
finishes and the
precision with which
materials meet

The shopfitting subsidiary of the Swiss-German furniture company Vitra is based in a humdrum 1950s office block which was transformed through the addition of a canopied glass and steel access bridge, opposite. Floodlit at night, overleaf, the glass steps seem to float in the landscape

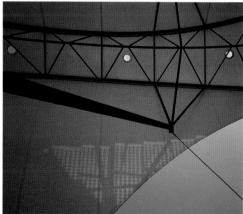

One of the most
ambitious projects
to date is an unbuilt
scheme for a new four-
storey headquarters
for Vitra in Basle,
below and overleaf.
An external supporting
structure and intricate
system of blinds, right
and opposite, would
have given the facades
a distinctive character

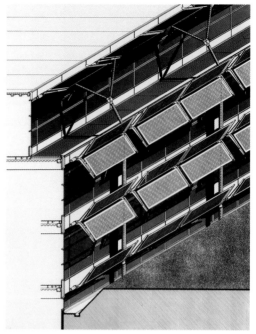

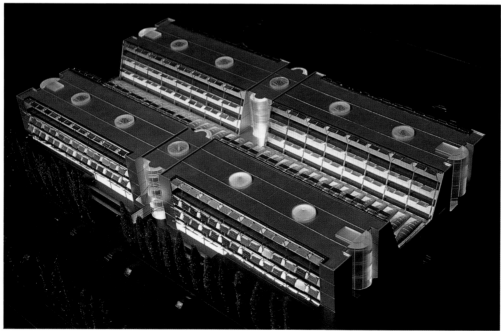

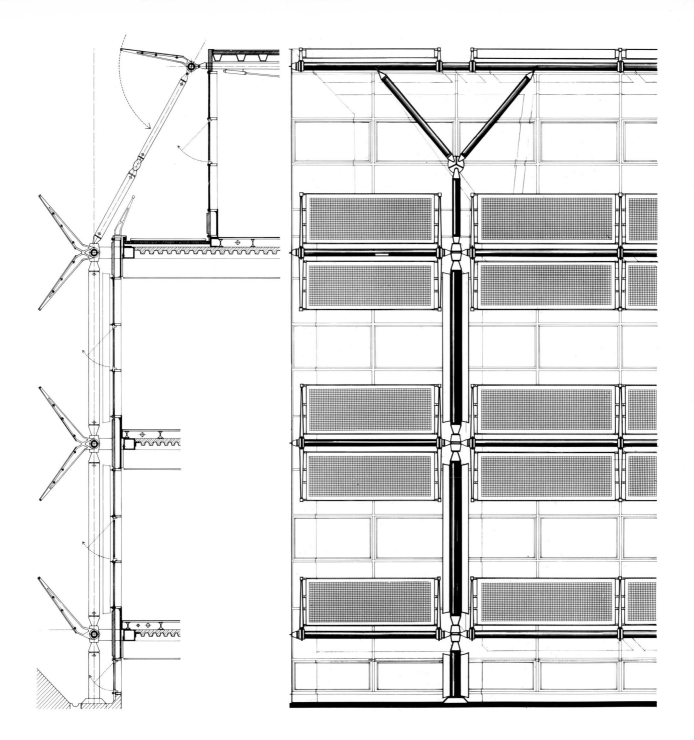

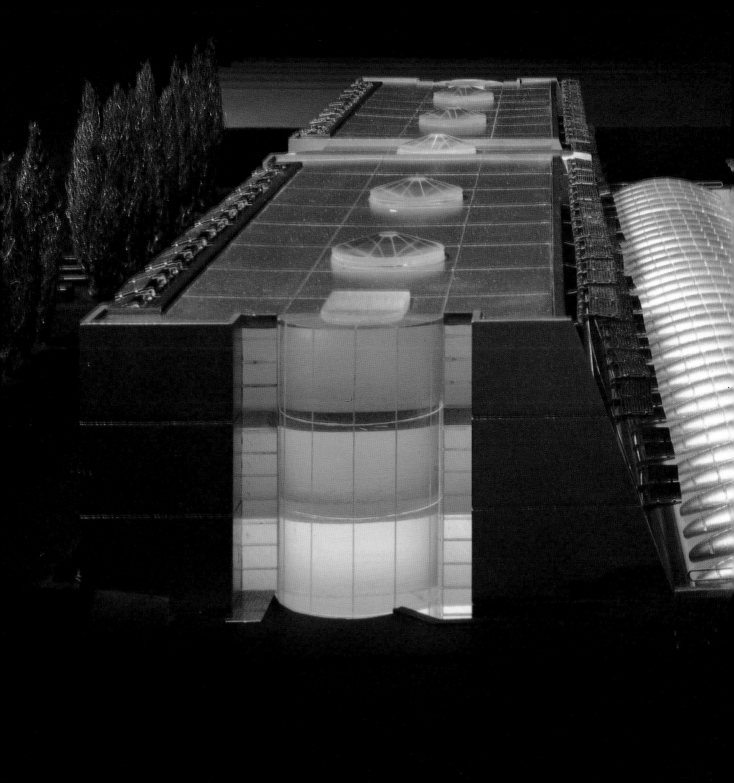

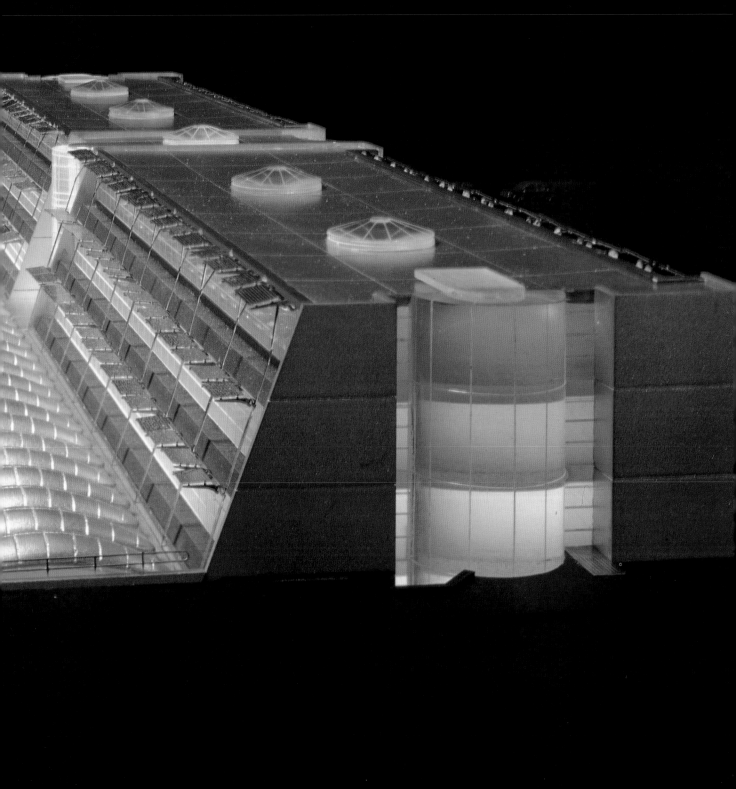

When Joseph Ettedgui
took over what had
once been the first
Habitat store in
London's Fulham Road,
he wanted to create
an interior with more
the character of a
department store
than a boutique. The
subdued polished
plaster finishes and
fluted columns, below,
provide a muted
setting which allows
the staircase, with
its glass treads and
spidery steel rods,
right and opposite,
to stand out as
a gravity-defying
conjouring trick

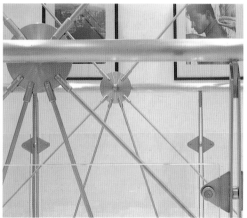

Design in Exile

In the three-storey Sloane Street Joseph shop, the staircase, refined to a bare minimum, forms the centrepiece of the interior. It has been designed as a piece of architecture in its own right, with its own structural logic and formal language

The interiors for Jardine Insurance's City of London offices, designed in collaboration with Michael Hopkins, gave the company a cool and sophisticated identity. The high-gloss finish of the staircase, right and opposite, transforms engineering into jewellery. The sail screens, below, are familiar from earlier projects, but as always are used in a slightly different way

The worldwide fashion chain Esprit has stores designed by Ettore Sottsass, Shiro Kuramata, Foster Associates and Antonio Citterio. EJA's unit for the company is in the Whiteleys building in London, a shopping centre carved out of a former department store. A bold use of stainless steel, opposite, gives the shop a powerful presence without it intruding into the mall on to which it faces

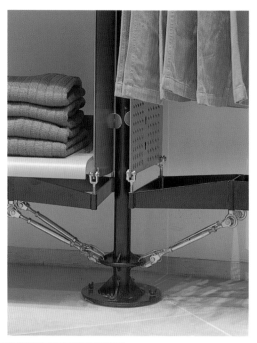

Simplicity is not Simple

For the refurbishment
of Legends nightclub
in 1987, left, polished
perforated aluminium
was used for the
staircase treads and
the central columns

"When you design for something that changes as quickly as fashion, you can't change the environment as quickly as the collections. Among other things you need something timeless. And if you look at history to see what has always been acceptable, it's black and white. Our job when we are designing a shop or an office is to produce a background. We are not producing a monument." Eva Jiricna, 1989

Like a worker in a socialist state, Eva Jiricna wears a uniform. It has variations, but in 1990 it tended to be dominated by a tailored black jacket with a pink handkerchief in the breast pocket carefully folded to support an 0.2 Rapidograph drawing pen which rises from its centre like the stamen of a flower. This arrangement has a semiological significance. The Rapidograph establishes professional credentials in a stylish sort of way. The pink handkerchief says woman. The black jacket is more enigmatic; perhaps it says European.

Most of the work of Eva Jiricna Architects consists of small jobs in big cities for rich clients. That is a simple way of describing the apartments, shops and offices the practice designs. But simple as it is to describe, such a professional life is filled with complexity and variation. The short contract periods that lie at the heart of it are punctuated by invitations to compromise, lose the initiative in a sea of detail and sacrifice the original clarity of an idea. Besides, as Eva Jiricna says, "Once you start doing small jobs it takes a miracle to move on to big ones."

But then again there are small jobs and small jobs. Like a prime-time commercial that is not only the shortest but also the most expensive programme on television, any one of EJA's shop designs can easily turn out to be an epic consumer of financial and design resources in relation to its size. Most of the shops EJA designs are small and most of the remodelling work that creates them is completed in a short time, but these are not small jobs in the sense that most architects understand that term. The moment the client leases the shop unit he or she starts paying a high rent, so it is futile to attempt to resist the pressure for an early completion. In the kind of retail work in which EJA specialises, three months from commissioning to completion is considered generous; two months more usual. The two-storey Joseph shop on London's Fulham Road that was opened in 1988 was on site three weeks after the client obtained the old Conran Habitat premises in which it was built. All such work is specialised, as well as being dominated by the state of the economy and the tide of consumer spending, so that not only can several commissions arrive at once, but so can competition for subcontractors capable of carrying out the work become intense as well.

The idea that these small jobs are located in big cities is equally misleading. Once a commission is secured, the city in which it is located fades into the background and all attention must be focused on the tiny volume of the particular apartment or shop that is to be built or remodelled. The influence of the city is felt only through its distance from London, the accessibility of the site by air or car or taxi, and the attitude of its building control bureaucracy to what is proposed. At the time of writing EJA has designed twelve Joan & David shoe shops in shopping streets and malls in Europe and the United States. Joan Helpern, the graduate psychologist shoe-designer who is the Joan in the name, is under no illusions about what is entailed. In 1988, when Eva Jiricna had designed only six shops for her, she was asked by American *House and Garden* magazine whether she would be designing more. "If she holds up she will," was Helpern's grim answer.

The popular idea that it might be easy to work for rich clients turns out to be an illusion too. The fact that a client may be a wealthy individual does not mean that he or she will want to spend a lot of money. More importantly, just because the client is an individual and not a committee or a corporate representative, he or she will seldom work bankers' hours and will always reserve the right to reverse decisions at any stage of the work. Such oscillations of opinion are not governed by ordinary budgetary constraints, nor by old-fashioned business conventions like the prompt payment of fees. Eva Jiricna has worked for shop clients who have started out placing a low limit on the cost of a staircase, and then at a very late stage approved the expenditure of ten times that amount on a staircase of an entirely different design, just because it caught their imagination. Conversely, she has endured delays in the payment of fees of up to two years, patiently waiting for the moment when the cheque will be written out.

"It is a matter of intuition," she explains of the budgetary uncertainty. "In most cases what the client wants bears no relation to the amount of money they say they are prepared to spend, so you have to guess how important their initial concept is to them and explain that to achieve it they will have to spend the money. On the other hand, if they want to hold back you have to have something ready for that too." The self-made super-rich rely on their own judgment where design is concerned and, unlike a corporate executive, they will exercise it without fear of the effect upon other parties. But they are not immune to advice. In Eva's opinion most of her clients are more susceptible to the convictions of others than sure of what they want themselves. "In general," she says, "people buy on recommendation; they are told that this is good, that is bad. They do not buy out of an innate aesthetic understanding of what is proposed. What they believe in is confidence, and that is both good and bad. In some ways we have benefited from the fact that many of them have no confidence when it comes to colour. If we had proposed a pink wall to them they might have got scared. But instead what we provide is a neutral background the client can add to later in small ways. And black and white is neutral, and therefore very safe."

One remarkable example of confidence that Eva cites concerns a former client whose art-historical reference system comprised only two style descriptors: "Hoffmann" and "Art Deco". This person repeatedly identified "Hoffmann" and "Art Deco" elements in the most unlikely places, on one occasion telephoning from the American mid-West with the news that there was a great deal of "Hoffmann" architecture there. Joseph Ettedgui, the fashion designer and retail entrepreneur whose patronage contributed crucially to the opening stages of Eva Jiricna's solo career, had no formal training in architecture or design, but started out as a hairdresser. "He has what is called a perfect eye," recalls Eva loyally. "If you do something that you know is right, he will appreciate it immediately. Joseph always wanted to become an architect and he tried hard to communicate that desire through me – I made it possible by listening very carefully without inhibiting his seemingly 'crazy' ideas. I tried to have the patience to change everything hundreds of times. But when he was my client he used my cultural references. I remember when I first asked him how he operates as a designer he said he just found the right people to copy. I was appalled. It took me a long time to understand what he meant."

Fashion entrepreneur Joseph Ettedgui, Eva Jiricna's early patron

Opposite: The Legends
staircase provides a
stage for socialising.
A bridge at mezzanine
level links the two
curving flights of stairs

Eva Jiricna established her reputation in the retail world by sharing her cultural references with Joseph Ettedgui. She had never done interiors before she met him and most of her real architecture had been unexecuted paper engineering in industrial materials of the kind that dominated the Brighton Marina drawings. The black, white and stainless steel that identified her work all over London in the 1980s came from this background, but in an indirect, osmotic fashion. It was an architecture created from a combination of native talent as a designer, a sense of order and restraint inherited from her Czech functionalist father, and the strange experience of the Marina and the informal apprenticeship she underwent there in the use of high-tech marine materials. This last element may always be imponderable. In many ways, her relationship with ships and boats at Brighton in the 1970s might be compared to that of Le Corbusier with aviation in the 1920s, a world that he appreciated not by making long flights, but by looking at pictures of aeroplanes and somehow drawing their shapes into his buildings. Eva Jiricna too seized upon curious, unrelated elements from images of the yachts and pontoons whose logic she so appreciated. Transferred to a sophisticated urban environment, these elements gave her shop interiors a conviction and authority that spilled over into the merchandise, and that was what Joseph, who had previously believed he could only achieve this by using the "cultural references" of established architects, recognised at a very early stage.

The role of Joseph in the making of Eva Jiricna's career is difficult to overestimate but easy to misinterpret. Joseph gained a prodigy, but a prodigy far beyond his own imagining. In the years that followed their first collaboration, he successfully applied the Jiricna formula to furniture and food retailing in addition to clothes. In those same years Eva Jiricna accumulated an impressive body of work after years as a paper architect who had built virtually nothing. What she took from the relationship was a world reputation.

At one level it can be said that Eva Jiricna's success, and perhaps the continuing success of Modern design in the consumer industries when elsewhere it has fallen into disrepute, stems from the fact that its methodology relates well to all consumer processes, from office work to shopping, eating out and dancing, because they all require organisation

and reward order and method while penalising "irrationality". In that sense all post-Modern shops, for example, carry a burden that is not always adequately eased by an invisible armature of Modern servicing. In the case of fashion shops, there is enough irrationality in the merchandise alone. The design of the shop has to make order easier than disorder or it does not work.

"If you have method," says Eva, "you can design anything. Each big design decision splits down into smaller design problems. You solve each of these problems in turn and you have your result. The only question then is whether all these packages come together and blend into an inviting soup, or just look like the sum of their ingredients."

A clothes shop in an existing building, the kind of premises where Eva Jiricna's reputation was made, has perhaps twenty elements to design. There is the door, the display window or windows, the shelves and hanging rails, the counters, the sliding ladders, the stairs... All of them can be reduced to unintimidating proportions, or treated as letters in the alphabet soup of small design problems that Eva Jiricna talks about. But with growing expertise and experience (four shops in Sloane Street by 1985), it became possible for her to focus on each of these elements in turn and explore its function within the retailing machine. In many cases this had been done by others, but Eva Jiricna was the first to introduce tension cables to support shelves and display tables rather than merely decorating them. More recently she has started to use pivoted doors with no frames or architraves. "As an architect I was used to having to design every detail and I naturally thought that was how interior designers worked too," she has said of her early shop designs. Yet in the event it was her capacity to design every detail that rapidly separated her from the rest of the interior design community, and nowhere more decisively than in the development of the element that makes the crucial link between one retail floor and another, the staircase.

In architecture and design, where elements must be designed and produced separately yet fit together as though they were parts of a single organism on site, the appearance of simplicity can only be achieved by discipline and great attention to detail. The epitome of this achievement is the staircase, which links floors and can only do so with absolute conviction if it starts and finishes in exactly the right place. "There is no doubt

Overleaf: Legends is
on two storeys, with
a restaurant on the
ground floor and a bar
and dance floor in the
basement. The sinuous
staircase dominates
the interior

that the staircase can be the most complicated single element in a simple shop design. But it need not be," Eva says. "There have been many great architectural staircases in history, but in the present century and particularly during the years of austerity after 1945, it became more common to shut the staircase away, literally, in a cupboard, and cover it with carpet. This was partly to do with lack of imagination, partly to save space and money, but whatever the reason, it resulted in the under-exploitation of the most unique three-dimensional object in any interior of more than one floor. To me a staircase can be treated as a designed object. It has an extraordinary power to transform a space, yet it is not a standardised piece of furniture. Obviously for commercial reasons we have to make each staircase different, but we have also become more ambitious with each successive job. For me a staircase is an opportunity for invention and escapism, what the whole of architecture is for Michael Graves."

In fact a staircase designed by Eva Jiricna is no more escapist than the hard-nosed world of fashion into which it fits. As an object it is a microcosm of the creative struggle of any high-tech architect to make something that is culturally welcomed (so that it attracts no consumer opposition); conforms to a bewildering network of regulations governing fire and safety (so that it is not illegal to build it); is not so expensive that no one will pay for it, and yet uses materials and methods in a way that is elegant but not extravagant and has never been done before.

In the whole of Eva Jiricna's work there are two particularly spectacular staircases that epitomise her mastery of the genre as well as pointing the way towards refinements that she will certainly bring to fruition in the future. At the time of writing EJA has designed over twenty staircases in Britain, France, Germany, Italy, Canada and the United States, all of them different, all of them original, but all of them including materials, methods or components that are reminiscent of one another. In a way they are as alike as, say, all the cars in the model range of BMW or Mercedes. But the two most innovative staircases Eva Jiricna has designed contain in some form elements from all the others. They are the 1987 curving steel and aluminium double stair at Legends nightclub and restaurant in Old Burlington Street and the stainless steel and glass triple stair for the large Joseph shop at 26 Sloane Street, completed in 1989.

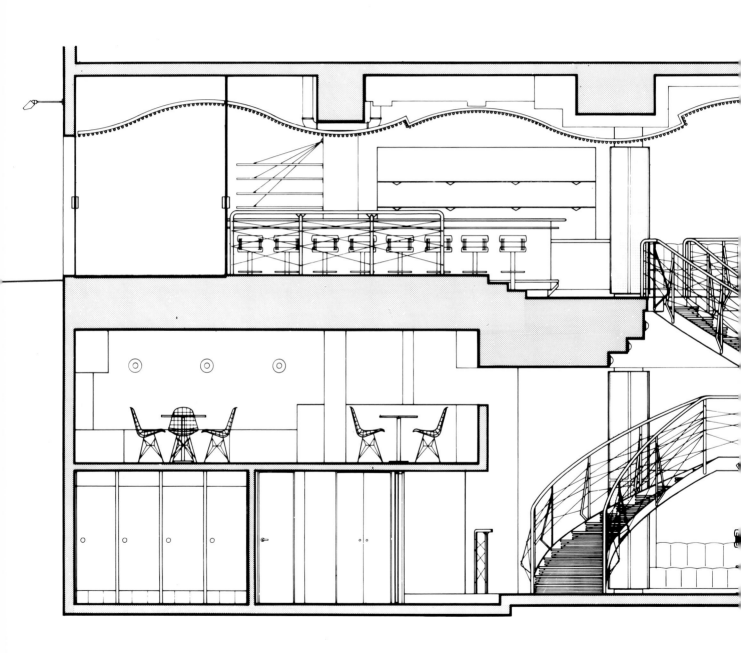

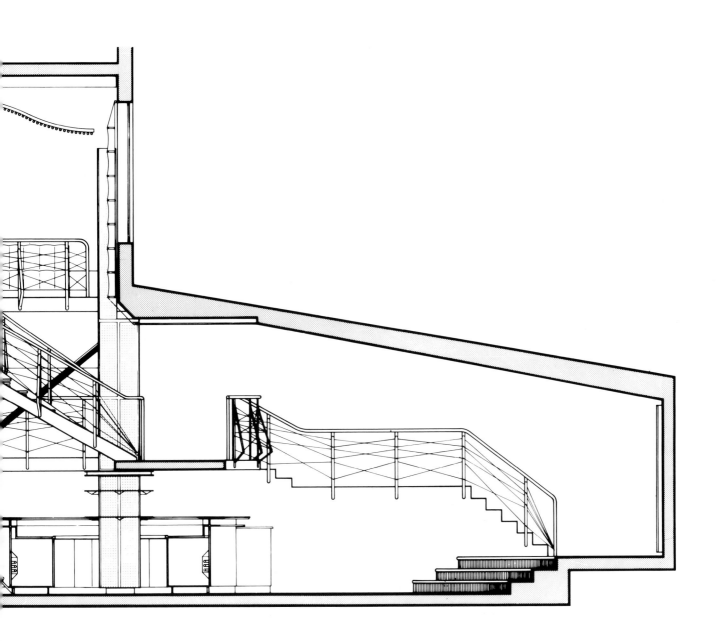

Opposite: The triple-flight staircase for the 1989 Joseph shop in Sloane Street takes the transparency of the Legends staircase to a new extreme

The Legends staircase is a classic because it demonstrates the genius of the architect in using geometry to evoke order from unpromising surroundings. Legends consisted of an inconveniently shaped ground floor and basement property broken up by large and obtrusive columns. In order to provide a focal point and a means of linking the two levels, EJA proposed a curving upper flight of stairs leading down to a mezzanine level, with a bridge above a bar crossing to a lower flight that curved down beneath the first to reach the basement floor. These twin curves not only provided a formal focus to the shapeless interior, but permitted a visual link between the ground floor and basement while requiring the structural addition of only a single beam at mezzanine level.

But the construction of such a stair would not be easy. Not only would the inner and outer strings be of a different radius on each flight, but the current club and restaurant regulations governing the strength of the handrails and balusters called for a capacity to resist 4 kilonewtons of lateral pressure instead of the 1.4 kilonewtons normal in retail work. In the event, this colossal strength requirement was later relaxed, but the complexity of manufacture of the 20mm rolled steel strings was never overcome and they had to be fed into a rotary press at a carefully calculated angle to achieve the necessary precise curved form.

The treads and risers for the Legends staircase were designed to be bolted between the strings as built-up assemblies consisting of steel and aluminium elements. Each tread was formed from polished perforated aluminium running back from a nosing and flared upwards at the base of the riser. These treads were supported by a system of ingenious three-dimensional steel trusses called "butterflies" that consisted of horizontal and vertical lozenge-profiled elements spanning between the strings. In order to maintain the visual openness of the treads, the risers too were skeletal, consisting only of two equally spaced steel tubes.

The balusters bolted to the inner and outer strings continued the theme of strength allied to transparency. Beneath a stainless steel tubular handrail, a series of vertical stainless steel bars descended to the string. These bars were braced on their outer face by another "butterfly" truss, this time of increasing horizontal depth from the handrail downwards. The maximum depth of the truss thus built up was reached at the head of each string. Between these balusters runs a tracery of 4mm

stainless steel rigging cable tensioned into a three-dimensional cage pattern that effectively fills in the space between the widely spaced balusters without losing the impressive openness of the whole design. This system made it possible to manufacture separately the irregularly shaped handrail and the regular balusters.

The Legends staircase consumed a vast amount of design time – "hundreds of hours", according to Eva – and its fabrication, which had to be entrusted to two different firms with the consequence that until the last moment there was doubt that it would all fit together with the high tolerances demanded, was scarcely an economical proposition. But its impact was formidable. Only the best-informed critics noticed that, for all its complexity, it was precise enough to be assembled mechanically with countersunk stainless steel yacht bolts and neat set screws instead of being welded together. Even for those who did not understand its construction, it became possible for the first time to see what a high-tech staircase could do for an ill-proportioned, converted property with no other distinction than its address.

The greatest single difference between the Legends staircase and the staircase at Joseph's 1989 Sloane Street shop is in the relative mass of the two structures. Joseph links three floors where Legends joins only two and Joseph is straight where Legends is curved and disjointed, but both assemblies are about creating openness in closed planar buildings. At Joseph, the feat is magnified by a formidable ephemeralisation of the ingredients of the stair itself. Where Legends never quite shed the massiveness that was originally to have been required of its structure to comply with safety regulations, Joseph takes many of the same ingredients and thins them down to a spidery, almost transparent web of stainless steel, glass and perspex that achieves its strength sparingly in tension instead of heavily in compression.

The Joseph shop at 26 Sloane Street was acquired in May 1989 and opened in mid-September of the same year. Thus by EJA's standards the contract period was relatively long, but the three-storey shop presented complications, with a different plan on every floor and the bulk of the retailing space above ground level. The staircase was conceived as a means of unifying these disparate elements. It is a triple straight-flight structure with landings, suspended vertically from specially strengthened first-floor and ground-floor ceilings. It is of extreme regularity, being on axis with the ground-floor entrance to the shop. Though resembling in some details the staircase in the smaller Joseph shop in Fulham Road, it is far larger and more complex. Because it is the only overtly high-tech feature in the whole interior of the Sloane Street shop, it achieves more completely what Eva Jiricna believed was possible when she first thought of "bringing out" the stair as a distinct designed object in itself, "like a car" in her own words, "like a jewel" in the words of one of her clients. As with the staircase at Legends, the Joseph staircase is truly a separate object because it can be disassembled and removed. Like the Legends staircase too it absorbed an immense amount of design time, its final cost being one-eighth of the price of the whole shop.

In the structural design of this staircase, as with much of their work over the past two years, EJA was aided by structural engineer Matthew Wells. Wells, recommended by pioneer high-tech engineer Tony Hunt, has an ability to work fast and to miniaturise complex structural solutions that conforms perfectly to EJA's work method and market. Together, EJA and Wells came up with a staircase that consists of intricate trusses supported between four stainless steel tensile supporting rods that are themselves diagonally braced vertically and horizontally by more steel rods of a smaller diameter. The solid steel strings of the Legends staircase are replaced by a pair of the most slender possible continuous steel rods linking all the tread nosings and tread tails along the pitch of every flight. Bracing between these steel rod strings, and joining them at set-bolted nodes at the nose and tail of each tread, are diagonal struts that, coupled with the complex structure of the treads themselves, convert this spidery assembly into a space frame. Braced off from this frame by short spacing rods, secured like the bottlescrews of a racing yacht with split pins, are the balusters supporting the handrails. Like those at Legends, these balusters are actually trusses themselves, but their structure is so light and the lateral displacement of their stiffeners so tiny that they would hardly be recognised as the same thing. The glass infill panels that occupy the spaces between the handrail and the upper chords of the space frame strings – equivalent to the cat's cradle of tension wires at Legends – are not directly supported by these balusters, for their lower fixings are located directly on to and through the treads, and their upper

Opposite: The
intensively engineered
treads of the Joseph
Sloane Street staircase
resolve the structural
forces at work in
the whole design

fixings to the slim double tube handrail itself. In this way any lateral load that they may have to withstand is conveyed to the main structure of the stairs.

At the heart of the design are the treads themselves. This time there are no risers, not even vestigial tubes, and the strings have been reduced to a bird cage of tiny struts, so the treads perform the final structural role of resolving the forces at work on the whole assembly. As a consequence the treads are a remarkably intensively engineered feature of the design. Where at Legends an all-metal built-up truss supported each perforated aluminium tread, at Joseph the treads are truly transparent, being formed in 20mm plate glass sandblasted in strips for friction and visibility. These glass treads rest on transparent perspex bearers of equal size to prevent glass falls in the event of an accidental breakage. It is this sandwich structure, whose deflection is minimised by a pair of circular stainless steel pads held in place by tensile "bowstrings" of rod-rigging, that enables the whole tread assembly to act as a compression member within the structural system of the stair.

No verbal description of the Joseph staircase can convey the sensation of delight at its astonishing transparency and surprise at its total rigidity that a visit to the shop will provide. The rest of the interior is a muted setting of natural grey plaster and discreet shelving that acts solely as a foil to this central feature, an element whose domination of the smaller ground floor is difficult to exaggerate. Yet dominant or not, the staircase is not a useless ornament because it also works in retail terms. Visually it is a void, so transparent in its structure that it acts as a window to allow a synoptic view of three separate floors of merchandise.

Six years before the design of the staircase at Joseph, Eva Jiricna remodelled an apartment for herself in Belsize Park. Excluding her work at Lloyd's, which might have led to a breakthrough on a different scale and of an entirely different kind had it been brought to fruition, this small flat, sold in 1988 and replaced by a larger, still unfinished Maida Vale successor, represents perhaps the greatest contrast with the classic restraint and discipline demonstrated at 26 Sloane Street.

At Belsize Park, as with most of the shop units with which she has had to deal in London, Eva Jiricna was faced with a small, irregularly shaped, dark space in an existing building. She also confronted a more

than usually limited budget. The flat itself, on the top floor of a seventy-year-old apartment block, was a four-roomed unit with no balcony or view and an inconvenient bathroom and kitchen arrangement. Partly by the use of glass in the form of mirrors, but mainly through a formidable functional ingenuity in the zoning of space and the careful planning of storage, she transformed this unprepossessing dwelling into an expression of the reconciliation between work and life that today informs her professional personality and confirms her independence.

The organisation of this apartment explains much about the relationship with objects that lies at the core of Eva's or any other architect's ability to create built environments in the material world. At Belsize Park the flat was divided into three separate zones. One where food preparation and personal hygiene were logically combined, back to back, behind sliding doors. A second where a small living room was enormously expanded in apparent size by the use of a wall of full-height mirrored cupboards with black-painted perforated steel spider braces to open them. And a third where a drafting table, a cantilevered television set, a narrow perforated metal desk with a typewriter, and cable-tray shelving mounted on an unboltable Dexion frame all shared the perimeter of a central space dominated by a Wink chair and a large plan chest with a bed on top of it – this last an innocent indication of priorities reminiscent of a passage in Frank Lloyd Wright's *Autobiography* in which he recalls the architectural apprentices of his youth sleeping on their drawing boards in the office at night.

In the way that Eva planned this apartment we can see the externalisation of her method, which calls for the breaking down of large design tasks into the answers to smaller design problems, and then the combination of these answers into a creative whole. Yet in the combination of ruthless zoning and negligible structural alteration to which the apartment was subjected we can see something else as well. Just as she was drawn to the Brighton Marina project years before because "in Czechoslovakia we have no sea", so is there a leitmotif of bright green studded rubber in the apartment because in the city there is no green. And deeper still is the thought that, while it may be ingenious and economical to redesign a flat without making any structural alterations, it is not strictly necessary to avoid them unless lack of money, the need for

Overleaf: The muted
setting of the Joseph
Sloane Street shop
allows the staircase
to stand out like a
piece of jewellery

speed, or the restrictive terms of a lease compel it. At Belsize Park any or all of these reasons might have applied, but they probably did not. It is more likely that neither poverty nor speed played as large a part in determining what should not be done as the deep inner conviction of impermanence that came from the life and beliefs of the designer. In truth only the exile and the emigré can experience this conviction and Eva Jiricna has been both of these. It is a kind of alienation that leads to an understanding of the provisional nature of all human arrangements, and one that can prosper in architecture only in specific fields like retailing or entertainment, where uncertainty is the first and most important rule of the game.

The Belsize Park apartment was featured in the April 1984 issue of the magazine *Architectural Design*. When Eva explained in its pages, using her own drawings and captions, that apparent space was to be created by the use of mirrors; that the seating area was to be convertible into a bedroom; that in her studio/bedroom her bed was to be "raised above the plan chest"; and that the walls were to be "covered with foam-backed linoleum to avoid replastering", she was inadvertently laying bare the central role of a conviction of impermanence in her entire creative process. For as we look at the plans of this efficiency apartment we suddenly realise that there is no conceptual difference between a bed "raised above the plan chest" and an epic steel and glass staircase that can be taken to pieces in three hours with a screwdriver, a pair of pliers and an Allen key. And if there is no difference there, then neither is there a conflict between the idea of such an architecture and the life of its originator: a designer born in the last days of a twenty-year republic; raised at the dead centre of a war that shook a continent to its foundations; trained under an extinct regime; now famous in the fashionable quarters of a dozen cities united only by a tide of conspicuous consumption.

There is, as the psychologist Carl Jung said, a "style" that links all the actions of every individual. As they win their victories so they endure their defeats. Only repeated actions have meaning. Only geometry is logical. Only reflections are true.

In the work of Eva Jiricna there is both genius and sadness. True to the Czech functionalist tradition, her architecture is instrumental, not monumental.

The Architecture of Reason

"Architecture is a very difficult subject to understand. It involves so many disciplines and practically everything in one way or another is linked to it. Nobody can possibly have all the necessary knowledge at hand to do everything right – it is a constant learning process."
Eva Jiricna, *Woman's Own*, 1988

When Eva Jiricna accepted an invitation from the mass-circulation magazine *Woman's Own* to oppose the writer Douglas Keay in a debate about the role of Prince Charles in architecture, she joined a select group of architects: those with the courage to speak out in defence of Modernism about the damage the Prince was doing to the careers of architects everywhere. Her contribution to the debate was simple but effective. It consisted of a defence of the expertise within the profession, combined with a plea for the acknowledgment of the role of experiment in the accumulation of objective human knowledge. Thus far would she go in her defence of Modern architecture to the public at large, but no further.

Yet within the architectural community, Eva Jiricna is unsparing when her critical judgment is sought. And never more so than when discussing the work of contemporaries whose design ethos she shares. In conversations about buildings, she can be as uncompromising as any Czech functionalist of her father's generation.

The Captain's Room, the basement restaurant of Richard Rogers' Lloyd's building, was one of the few parts of Eva Jiricna's designs for the interior of the building to be realised

**The clear central
atrium of Richard
Rogers' Lloyd's building**

For example in speaking of Richard Rogers' Lloyd's building, to which she made her own contribution in the shape of the omnipresent black light fittings, the design of the underwriters' boxes and the interior of the original Captain's Room restaurant, she once told a BBC presenter: "It is a mad idea, but it is still the best building around." This opinion was voiced in connection with a poll carried out to discover the views of selected high-tech architects on the best buildings of the 1980s. Eva voted Rogers' epic structure the best non-residential building of the decade. But what did she mean by "mad idea"?

"I think Richard Rogers was mistaken in trying to create a clear, open serviced space in the interior of the building, in view of the cost of this decision in other ways," she begins. "Having experienced the difficulties of working in steel at the Pompidou Centre in Paris, he tried to build Lloyd's in concrete. But the clear flexible space he achieved in plan was at the expense of a massive coffered concrete floor system in section, resulting in a building that is extremely tall but has relatively few floors. The often commented-on oppressive effect in the interior of storeys of a far from enormous floor-to-floor height stacked on top of one another is a result of the architects' attempt to deal with this problem. Each floor plate may have very few supporting columns, but it is made up of concrete members almost 1 metre deep that are horizontally hardly pene-

The all-glass elevation of Foster Associates' office building at Stockley Park

trable to servicing. Once you add the depth of a raised floor above that to provide the horizontal service space you need, you have a depth of something like 1.6 metres for every serviced floor in the building."

She is similarly logical in her analysis of a different range of problems that arose at the Foster Associates buildings at Stockley Park and Albert Wharf, where enamel dots on glass, a process called "fritting", was used as part of the cladding system. In both cases, the "fritting" on its own not only proved inadequate as a means of protection against heat gain, but generated annoying shadow "dotting" on the workstations inside the building. Again Eva's view is that this shortcoming in design logic was the result of a struggle for perfection in one area at the expense of ignoring other problems. "The architects must have been in the grip of a wish-fulfilment. Foster Associates wanted to achieve an all-glass elevation at a low price at Stockley, so they compromised in other areas to get one."

Such criticisms invite a *tu quoque* response. What would EJA have done confronted with the same design problems? The answer may well have been along the lines of the project for a new £5 million, 5,000 square metre headquarters building for the Swiss furniture company, Vitra, in Basle, for which EJA, working in conjunction with engineers Dewhurst MacFarlane, had completed the designs when it was unexpectedly cancelled by Vitra's president, Rolf Fehlbaum, in the spring of 1990. Although a much smaller job than Lloyd's and only a little larger than Stockley, the Vitra brief contained variants of the Lloyd's building height limit problem and the Stockley glass cladding problem. Both of these were solved by EJA by means of an enterprising piece of design, though Eva is at pains to point out that it is an unbuilt project, and "God knows what else might have gone wrong."

The task of EJA at Vitra was to accommodate a large amount of serviced floor space below an overall height limit imposed by neighbouring buildings and to control heat gain and provide privacy behind an exposed glass facade. The answer the firm came up with had as its starting point an extremely thin steel floor system offering maximum horizontal servicing space, with outrigged structural supports rather than outrigged servicing towers as at Lloyd's. In the case of the cladding, EJA provided for floor-to-ceiling tinted glass, but combined with large external perforated metal angled sun screens to control overlooking and heat gain.

The manner in which this combination of design innovations would have worked is a classic example of the process of synergetic reinforcement, or multiplying advantage, that can be achieved in architecture by a logical and resourceful designer. The first advantage gained from outrigging the vertical elements of the structural frame was a reduction in the amount of fireproofing needed, simply because these elements would no longer confront such high temperatures in the event of a fire. The second advantage was that because the structure was outside the glass cladding envelope, it was in the right position to support the substantial array of sun screens needed to control heat gain and avoid problems of privacy – both matters conventionally dealt with either inside the building with a penalty in the form of lost floor space, or outside the envelope at the cost of providing expensive additional external support structures. What Eva Jiricna modestly describes as "a limited, logical simplification of a problem" would have made an important contribution to the evolution of advanced technology buildings everywhere.

Being of wholly European education and training, Eva does not trace such daring developments of Modern Movement reductionist thinking back to US origins in the writings and experiments of the design guru Richard Buckminster Fuller, though she does recognise Fuller's formulation of the need for a "more-for-lessing-design science revolution" as allied to the guiding principles that governed the pre-war development of Czech functionalist thought. In Eva's view, it is the duty of all rational architects everywhere to design for the minimum expenditure of energy and resources, to use logic in problem analysis and advanced materials and methods in construction, all in order to do more with less. Despite her denial of a direct Fuller influence, there is indisputable evidence in her work of this process of "ephemeralisation" (as Buckminster Fuller named it after the Greek *ephemeros*, meaning lasting only for a day) to be seen in even her most expensive retail interiors. The stainless steel rigging wires used to support staircases, window displays and shelves can be considered a more-for-lessing EJA innovation, but they do have antecedents. A foretaste of them can be seen in the ingenious fitted wardrobes and shelves in Buckminster Fuller's Wichita House, a prefabricated dwelling designed to be assembled on aircraft production lines, of which two prototypes were made in 1945.

Architects like Norman Foster, Richard Rogers, Michael Hopkins and Eva Jiricna could perhaps be expected to agree about the desirability of the guiding principle of ephemeralisation, although all perhaps with one reservation or another. But their reasons would be different. Foster worked closely with Fuller for a time; Hopkins has been known to remark that he "put all that Bucky stuff in the bank years ago". More importantly, all four are architects of broadly the same generation and none of them has either wholly repudiated the Modern basis of their training, or the place of logic in their design process.

But in the case of Eva Jiricna, there is another side to the question of rationality. By a strange irony, EJA's Vitra headquarters building was probably cancelled because of cost overruns on another Vitra commission, a company museum and art gallery by the wayward Californian architect Frank Gehry that stemmed from an entirely different design tradition. Eva is not altogether enthusiastic about Gehry's architecture although there are curious echoes of her own work in his use of industrial materials and serendipitously chosen objects. Eva's old Belsize Park apartment, for example, boasted suction plate glass lifters as door handles and cable trays as shelves; Gehry's Los Angeles home uses cheap expanded metal, steel mesh reinforcing and even aircraft parts. But where Gehry *applies* industrial materials to his buildings and does not trouble himself overmuch about the elegance of their junctions one with another, Eva Jiricna *integrates* such materials into the image of a logical machine-made whole. It is because of this difference that she relegates Gehry's idiosyncratic buildings, along with those of all the post-Modernists and classical revivalists that she has encountered, to a category loosely defined as "irrational". Such architecture is not subject to the same rational critique she applies to her own work. In fact, in her view, its very waywardness stems from the way in which it has managed to make itself "idiot-proof" by claiming an immunity to logical criticism.

Eva Jiricna has thought deeply about the role of this pervasive "irrationality" in architecture. Ultimately she is not as negative about it as one might expect. In part this may be because as a pragmatist and not a theorist, she recognises that it is already a force to be reckoned with in the public perception of architecture. But in part too her permissiveness proceeds from her view of what is real and what is apparent progress.

"I believe that progress occurs when experiments take place above the average level of technological sophistication," she says. "That is to say, when ideas, materials, methods, or any combination of these, advance beyond the conventional wisdom of the construction industry. Now it would be wonderful if this always occurred in connection with worthy causes – it was the Czech writer, Karel Capek, who said, 'Mankind will stay in misery until it learns to cope with the most essential tasks first' – but that does not often happen. In practice, invention occurs where someone is broad-minded enough to permit it, and it does not occur where they are not. I can sympathise with people who find the spectacle of invention confined to the service of wealthy commercial clients repulsive in its way, almost unacceptable. But in my case it enables me, for instance, to design and build a staircase costing as much as a house, and however irrelevant such a thing may appear to the important issues of our time, that is a kind of freedom. It is the same kind of freedom that the 'irrational' post-Modernists and revivalists enjoy in the design of whole buildings. However wayward what they do may be, it is still the result of imagination having been permitted to operate above the average level."

This capacity to see virtue in the massive flirtation with historical architecture and undisciplined stylistic abandon that has occurred in the years since her father's death is a considerable intellectual feat. It enables her to dismiss the "irrational" at a serious intellectual level, while still granting it the right to exist, indeed to achieve things, in the name of creative freedom. This is perhaps the only appropriate position for an emigré who left her country in pursuit of her own creative freedom to take, but it is by no means *carte blanche* for critical approval.

"People brought up in a thoroughly traditional environment like Buckingham Palace or a public school can airily say: 'Technology can make it work'. But they don't know *which* technology, or even what 'technology' is. Of course it is *possible* to build buildings that look like Renaissance masterpieces out of light alloys, plastics and other high-tech materials. But whether it is right to do such a thing in our time and, more importantly, whether any of the classical revivalists *actually knows how to do it* is another matter. To me all classical revival buildings look like obvious fakes. They never make good their boast about technology and the illusion of genuine age. It is not 'technology' that makes everything all right in architecture, but tender loving care for the project and an immense study of materials and methods. Without these nothing can be 'made all right' by anybody.

"As for Quinlan Terry, I know he actually believes in traditional materials and hand craftsmanship, perhaps as a kind of job-creation system of architecture. But his Richmond Riverside development – for which we were invited to design a shop, except that they wanted it with bull's eye windows and Georgian details so we refused – also looks to me like a fake. In a way it is like the reconstruction of the centre of Warsaw after 1945, except that I can accept that, because it was the replacement of a historic monument that had been tragically destroyed, even if it was not at all 'faithfully done' as is claimed. But Richmond is not the restoration of an ancient monument. It is not Modern. It is not classical. It is classically incompetent.

"When I was a student we were made to draw the classical orders. All of my father's generation was too. The great Modern pioneers knew classical detailing and classical proportions from their student days. Why is it that today the people who are building these new generation classical buildings, and even running special schools under royal patronage to teach more people how to do it, are actually so deeply incompetent themselves?

"In my opinion students should be taught history and only history. But the future should be open to the imagination. Nobody should try to legislate for that. In my own lifetime I have seen the futility of trying to do so."

Of the American architect Robert Venturi she is more pitying than hostile. "All I can say about the National Gallery extension is that it looks ugly. But I know enough about his earlier work to say that it was not done in a naive or irresponsible spirit." Of Michael Graves, another architect whose inspiration and method has little in common with her own, she will concede that "he has given the level of imagination another dimension", yet groups him as part of the whole, to her mind, unsuccessful adventurism of post-Modernism. A failure because it is a failure of nerve. "Post-Modernism is no more than an incompetent answer to the problem that Modernism did not solve, the problem of humanity in architecture," is her summation.

Eva Jiricna's conviction that these twentieth-century "irrationalists" have made things easy for themselves by abandoning the "limited, logical simplification of problems" is reflected in her insistence that their work is objectively uncriticisable. "When Michael Graves designs he produces no pressure on anybody's knowledge. His work is not demanding or difficult to understand. His clients, his peers, his critics, none of them has to say even why they like what he has done, or why they don't like what he has done. Like Gehry, his designs generate problems that he leaves to be solved by experts in the construction industry – either that or they are ignored in order to achieve the visual effect he wants, irrespective of any penalties involved. I can understand how it works with their clients – nearly all clients would rather kill themselves than admit that they don't understand what their architect is talking about. And even if they did understand, what could they say? What is the point of a giant dolphin or a swan on top of a hotel? It is tasteless, a bad joke. The only point is the exercise of a kind of freedom that I have described. In the end such designs do not really contribute to material culture; they are an escape from it."

Why then did Modernism fail to solve the "human" problems of material culture?

"I think it was the misinterpretation of Modernism that failed. When the real Modernism began in the twentieth century it was the first architecture since ancient times that had the possibility to survive endlessly by interpretation the way that classical architecture had. Think of how it started. It brought light and air into dark and unhealthy slum cities. It helped women. It made the kitchen a pleasant place. It made it possible for a woman to lead a normal life, neither a driver of domestic slaves nor a domestic slave herself. It was simple, not confusing. It produced simple answers to complicated functional problems.

"Right up to the 1930s nobody could honestly say that Modern architecture had failed. Its buildings were designed by architects of great culture with great knowledge of materials and proportion and lifestyle. The buildings were comfortable; their designers worked with soft materials as well as hard. I defy anyone to say that Eileen Gray's furniture or Le Corbusier's villas did not have a classical sense of proportion and comfort. This architecture may not have been acceptable to everyone, but its influence was growing. If it had not been for the generational change, and the outbreak of the Second World War that prevented any construction for six years, its influence would have gone on and on growing. It was the war that displaced all the talented architects and impoverished their countries. What followed 1945 was the so-called Modern architecture that failed. The next generation, the cousins and second cousins of the real Modern architects, took over the profession, not only with no experience, but with what were essentially political, not architectural goals, however necessary these might have been. Goals like: 'set up factories to build 500,000 houses a year', or 'start twenty new towns'.

"In this atmosphere the subtlety and softness of the early Modern houses was lost. In just a few years the whole stratum of society that had produced them had disappeared. After 1945 it was technically possible to produce hundreds of houses like the Villa Fric in Prague by Ladislav Zak, built only ten years earlier. This was not a low-cost housing unit, but an expensive house in a Prague suburb, a reinforced concrete building with impeccable interpenetration of inside and outside space, a deep understanding of materials and, most of all, comfort. But after 1945 the architects of such houses were dispersed and the clients for such houses had disappeared. These houses were replaced by mass housing without any proper design development.

"I know things were that way in Britain too. I worked at the GLC and there I was told about men who came back from the war and were made section heads and given enormous housing projects to design without any experience at all, without even having completed their training. It was not simply a matter of lack of money: where architects who had been properly trained, had practical experience and practised with tender loving care were put in charge of jobs, the result was not a failure. I do not consider Roehampton a failure. The other day I passed Ernö Goldfinger's Trellick Tower. That still has presence. It is modelled, formed, it is not just a block of the kind that destroyed Modern architecture by its crudeness and insensitivity.

"I often think of the history of Modern architecture as a diagram, shaped like an inverted cone. At the bottom there is a narrow, strong, concentrated inspiration allied to great skill and knowledge; at the top there is a broad, weak, diluted level of undistinguished building. In the 1930s we were at the bottom; now we are at the top. And all the insensitivity of the post-war years in the public sector has now been passed on to the private sector as well. Developments like Broadgate seem to me the beginnings of a monster environment that is worse than anything that has gone before. At Canary Wharf the environment that is being created is almost indescribable. It is like a *nouveau riche* Disneyland, a wealthy, socially irresponsible, squash-playing money and jogging machine, completely segregated from the rest of the city.

"I still believe that Modern architecture can exist forever, by interpretation, so it will survive this period of weakness and confusion, but it will only do so by retrieving what was lost, by recovering the warmth and proportion that was thrown away by socialist realism in the East and now by the worst excesses of commercialism in the West. Nobody really knows how to do this. The only exercise worth doing is to try to find out.

"In architecture I am my own most severe critic. I have learned that in any project so many things go wrong that what turns out at the end is generally a mess. So whatever you try to do, you should do for your own conscience. Nothing else can guide you. If you tried to do what everybody told you to do, you would be in a lunatic asylum by the time you reached the age of thirty-five. True freedom is to try with each successive project to do something different and better. To try to absorb everything you can from the existing knowledge. To try each time to do something that has not been done before, or not been done so well before."

Eva Jiricna gained her independence the hard way. Twenty years ago, when she first came to London, she worked in the schools division of the Greater London Council, a vast bureaucratic organisation scarcely different in any important way from the University of 17 November or the Institute of Fashion and Industrial Design in Communist Czechoslovakia. Today she survives, running an international practice from her London office, while all three of these monster bureaucracies have ceased to exist. She perceives this paradox as an indication of the dramatic difference between the two separate stages of her life. The first a kind of slavery and the second a kind of freedom. And however strong her feelings for or against different approaches to architecture, against the privilege of that freedom she will never support censorship of any kind.

Way-In Harrods
Jan Kaplicky – Future
Systems
Chris Grasby
Kathy Kerr
Carolina Aivars
Peter Bernamont

Joseph pour la Ville
Alan Morris
Engineer: Tim MacFarlane
(Dewhurst MacFarlane)

Joe's Cafe
Tim Bushe
Carolina Aivars
Alan Morris
Mark Guard
Kathy Kerr

Legends
Jon Tollit
Chris Grasby
Mike Loates Taylor
Ian Faulkner
Engineer: Tim MacFarlane
(Dewhurst MacFarlane)

**Vidal Sassoon,
Frankfurt**
Peter Bernamont
Kathy Kerr
Carolina Aivars

**Joan & David,
San Francisco**
Jon Tollit
Duncan Webster
CJ Lim
Engineer: Matthew Wells
(Whitby & Bird)

**Joan & David,
Los Angeles**
Jon Tollit
Duncan Webster
Engineer: Matthew Wells
(Whitby & Bird)

Joan & David, Paris
Duncan Webster

Vitrashop offices
Jon Tollit
Tim Bushe
Carolina Aivars
Duncan Webster
Ivan Reimann
Ho Jai Cheung
Engineer: Tim MacFarlane
and Paul Nuttall (Dewhurst
MacFarlane)

Joseph, Fulham Road
Jon Tollit
Duncan Webster
Tony Sayers
Engineer: Matthew Wells
(Whitby & Bird)

**Joseph,
26 Sloane Street**
Jon Tollit
Duncan Webster
Huw Turner
Engineer: Matthew Wells
(Dewhurst MacFarlane)

Jardine Insurance
Robert Birbeck
Duncan Webster
Mark Mallindine
Jon Tollit
Engineer: Matthew Wells
(Whitby & Bird)

Esprit shop, Whiteleys
Duncan Webster
Carolina Aivars
Engineer: Matthew Wells
(Dewhurst MacFarlane)

1979
● Joseph shop, South Molton Street, London W1

1980
● Apartment for Joseph, Sloane Street, London SW1 (*AD* Project Award)
● Le Caprice restaurant, Arlington Street, London W1

1981
● Chinese Laundry shop, South Molton Street, London W1

1982
● Architect's own apartment, Belsize Park, London NW3
● Kenzo shop, Sloane Street, London SW1 (*AD* Project Award)
● Studies for the interior of Lloyd's (with Richard Rogers Partnership) including the design of the Captain's Room restaurant

1983
● Joseph Tricot shop, Sloane Street, London SW1
● Pour la Maison shop, Sloane Street, London SW1
● L'Express café, Sloane Street, London SW1
● Apartment for Joseph, Wadden Mews, London SW1
● Joseph Tricot shop, Rue Etienne Marcel, Paris

1984
● Formica ColorCore chair and table designs, The Boilerhouse, V&A, London SW7
● Joseph Bis shop, Sloane Street, London SW1

1985
● Ideal Standard Exhibition, The Building Centre, Store Street, London WC1
● Way-In, Harrods, London SW3 (with Future Systems)
● Levi Strauss exhibition stand

1986
● Joseph pour la Ville shop, Brompton Road, London SW3
● Joseph pour la Maison shop, Draycott Avenue, London SW3
● Joe's Cafe, Draycott Avenue, London SW3
● Vidal Sassoon Sanctuary, London WC1
● Express Foods exhibition stand
● Apartment, Tottenham Street, London W1
● Apartment, Chesham Place, London SW1
● Apartment, Callow Street, London SW3
● Levi Strauss exhibition stand

1987
● Legends nightclub, Old Burlington Street, London W1
● Fafalios shipping company, Baltic Street, London EC1 (office refurbishment and apartment)
● Vidal Sassoon hairdressing salon, Frankfurt
● Touring exhibition for the British Council
● Birger Christensen shop, Copenhagen airport
● Planet retail system
● Project for gallery extension, RIBA, London W1 (limited competition)
● Joan & David shoe shop, Harvey Nichols, London SW1
● Joan & David shoe shop, Ogilvys, Montreal
● Joan & David shoe shop, Creeds, Toronto

1988

- Apartment for the Thompson Twins, London SW18
- Birger Christensen shop, Copenhagen
- Birger Christensen shop, London
- Joan & David shoe shop, Union Square, San Francisco
- Joan & David shoe shop, South Coast Plaza, Los Angeles
- Alex boutique, Florence (Interiors Retail Award)
- Antonia boutique, Riccione
- Quintessence retail system for Vitra
- Project for new Underground station, Hillingdon, London (limited competition)
- Vitrashop, Weil-am-Rhein, Germany (office refurbishment and landscaping)
- Vitra Headquarters, Basle, Switzerland (commissioned design, unbuilt)
- Joseph shop, Fulham Road, London SW3
- Joan & David shoe shop, Rue Faubourg Saint-Honoré, Paris

1989

- Harabels boutique, Beauchamp Place, London SW3
- Joseph shop, 26 Sloane Street, London SW1
- Jardine Insurance Corporation, City of London, (office interiors, with Michael Hopkins)
- Esprit shop, Whiteleys, London W2
- Comme Çi Comme Ça shop, Whiteleys, London W2
- Office furniture system for Vitra
- Pembridge Mews, London W11 (mews house refurbishment)
- Retail system for Esprit, Europe

1990

- St Marks Church, North Audley Street, London W1 (proposed conversion into offices)
- 7-9 Paddington Street, London W1 (proposed conversion and extension of buildings in a conservation area into an office, retail and residential complex)
- "Devetsil" exhibition, The Design Museum, London and the Museum of Modern Art, Oxford
- Hairdressing salon for Neville Daniel, Basil Street, London SW3
- Trusthouse Forte, Montecarlo, Monaco, (hotel interiors)
- Joan & David shoe shops: 5th Avenue, New York Copley Place, Boston Short Hills, New Jersey Tower City, Cleveland Century City, Los Angeles Cherry Creek, Denver North Park, Dallas Chevy Chase, Washington Pacific First Center, Seattle
- Apartment, Rutland Gate, London SW7

Although a large number of magazine articles have been devoted to the work of Eva Jiricna Architects and the background of the firm's principal, most are extremely superficial. The background books and articles below are the most useful I have found.

R.H.Bruce Lockhart, *Retreat from Glory*, Putnam, 1934

"Eva Jiricna", *Architectural Design*, April 1984

Pilar Viladas, "Lean, not mean", *Progressive Architecture*, September 1986

"Black and white and Joseph all over", *Blueprint*, September 1986

Alvin Boyarsky, "Conversation with Eva Jiricna", *Eva Jiricna Designs*, Architectural Association Publications, 1987

Czech Functionalism 1918-38, exhibition catalogue compiled by Jan Kaplicky with an introductory essay by Vladimir Slapeta, Architectural Association Publications, 1987

"Jiricna's Mini Store", *RIBAJ Interiors*, January 1987

"Street Style", *British Design in the 80s*, 1987

Lance Knobel, "Legends Nightclub Staircase", *Designers' Journal*, April 1987

Jose Manser, "British Design", *Interiors*, March 1987

Richard Wilcock, "All Ship-shape", *RIBA Journal*, November 1987

Otakar Hlavacek, Miroslav Kouba, *Dialogues about Housing in Czechoslovakia*, Orbis, Prague, 1988

Robert Kee, *Munich: the eleventh hour*, Hamish Hamilton, 1988

"Perfect Partnership", *Drapers' Record*, 22 October 1988

"Joseph Steps Up", *Blueprint*, November 1988

"Portrait: Eva Jiricna", *Crée*, December 1988

"In the Mode", *Interiors*, January 1989

"Jiricna Bravura", *Architectural Review*, January 1989

"Joe's Dream Palazzo", *Designers' Journal*, January 1989

Jonathan Glancey, "Freedom to be Functional", *The Independent*, 2 December 1989

Hugh Aldersey-Williams, "Joseph Takes Steps", *Designers' Journal*, November/December 1989

Devetsil: Czech Avant-Garde Art, Architecture and Design in the 1920s and 1930s, Museum of Modern Art, Oxford and The Design Museum, London, 1990

Alan Blanc, "Worker Town" *Building Design*, 13 July 1990

John Welsh, "Sitting in the Shade", *Building Design*, Cladding supplement, March 1990

Gina and Jeremy Newsom, *Closely Observed Buildings*, BBC 2, June 1990